UNSPOKEN

ELLA F. WASHINGTON, PHD

UNSPOKEN

A GUIDE TO CRACKING THE HIDDEN CORPORATE CODE

Forbes | Books

Published by Forbes Books, Charleston, South Carolina.
An imprint of Advantage Media Group.

Forbes Books is a registered trademark, and the Forbes Books colophon is a trademark of Forbes Media, LLC.

Printed in the United States of America.

10 9 8 7 6 5 4 3 2 1

ISBN: 979-8-88750-491-9 (Hardcover)
ISBN: 979-8-88750-601-2 (Paperback)
ISBN: 979-8-88750-492-6 (eBook)

Library of Congress Control Number: 2024904231

Cover design by Analisa Smith.
Layout design by Ruthie Wood.

This custom publication is intended to provide accurate information and the opinions of the author in regard to the subject matter covered. It is sold with the understanding that the publisher, Forbes Books, is not engaged in rendering legal, financial, or professional services of any kind. If legal advice or other expert assistance is required, the reader is advised to seek the services of a competent professional.

Since 1917, Forbes has remained steadfast in its mission to serve as the defining voice of entrepreneurial capitalism. Forbes Books, launched in 2016 through a partnership with Advantage Media, furthers that aim by helping business and thought leaders bring their stories, passion, and knowledge to the forefront in custom books. Opinions expressed by Forbes Books authors are their own. To be considered for publication, please visit **books.Forbes.com**.

To my mother, Victoria Motley Washington.

Thank you for your unwavering support and unconditional love.

You are my inspiration.

Visit **www.ellafwashington.com** online to access these free resources and stay connected.

TAKE the "How Strong Is Your Career Playbook" Assessment

How strong is your career playbook? Do you carry purpose-driven values from one workplace to another, or do you find yourself adopting the values your employers and clients expect? Are you intentional about developing your skills to align with your goals? Take this short quiz to find out where you stand - **www.ellafwashington.com/assessment**

SUBSCRIBE to Workplace Utopia Newsletters

Ready to enhance your workplace experience? Subscribe to the Workplace Utopia Newsletter and unlock a world of valuable insights, tips, and resources tailored to empower your professional journey. Stay ahead of the curve and elevate your career to new heights. Join our community today! Subscribe now at **www.ellawashington.com/news-archive/.**

DOWNLOAD The Necessary Journey Resource Guide
(or Free Chapter)

Discover essential resources for your journey! Download "The Necessary Journey Resource Guide" and equip yourself with valuable insights to navigate your path to success. Start your journey now! Get your free chapter at **www.ellafwashington.com/downloads.**

BOOK Dr. Ella for Speaking Engagements

Ready to inspire your audience? Book Dr. Ella for your next event and ignite meaningful conversations that drive change and growth. Elevate your gatherings with expert insights and engaging presentations. Secure your booking today! Contact us at **www.ellawashington.com/speaking.**

STAY CONNECTED with Dr. Ella on LinkedIn

Expand your network and stay informed! Connect with Dr. Ella on LinkedIn to access exclusive content, industry insights, and networking opportunities. Join a community of like-minded professionals dedicated to continuous growth and collaboration. Connect now at **https://www.linkedin.com/in/ellafwashington/.**

SCAN ME

CONTENTS

ABOUT THE AUTHOR XI

INTRODUCTION 1

ASSESSMENT: 15

SECTION ONE 21

CHAPTER ONE 23
Own Your Story

CHAPTER TWO 47
The Power of Your Strengths

CHAPTER THREE 67
Authenticity and Code-Switching

SECTION TWO 91

CHAPTER FOUR **9 3**
Be Ready, Be Right, Be Excellent

CHAPTER FIVE **1 1 5**
Read the Room

CHAPTER SIX **1 3 7**
Expand Your Networks of Influence

SECTION THREE **1 6 3**

CHAPTER SEVEN **1 6 5**
Master the ABCs of Negotiation

CHAPTER EIGHT **1 9 1**
Lean In to Grow

CHAPTER NINE **2 0 5**
Create Your Own Niche

CONCLUSION **2 2 7**
Write Your Own Playbook

ACKNOWLEDGMENTS **2 5 9**

ENDNOTES **2 6 1**

APPENDIX OF UNSPOKEN RULES . . **2 8 3**

ABOUT THE AUTHOR

Dr. Ella F. Washington is the founder and CEO of Ellavate Solutions and the author of multiple books on diversity, equity, and inclusion. Dr. Washington is a professor of practice at Georgetown University's McDonough School of Business. A recognized authority in DEI, Dr. Washington has consulted with businesses across industries, including finance, energy, education, and government.

For nearly twenty years, organizational psychologist Dr. Ella F. Washington has dedicated her life to "Elevating Humanity in the Workplace" by making the workplace a better, healthier, more equitable space for everyone. As the founder and CEO of Ellavate Solutions, a professor of practice at Georgetown University's McDonough School of Business, and an in-demand consultant, speaker, and expert on workplace issues, Dr. Washington works with everyone from students to CEOs on issues including women in the workplace, barriers to inclusion for diverse groups, and the construction of more inclusive corporate cultures. In her book *Unspoken*, she takes her efforts directly to workers struggling to find their way in a corporate world that may not have been made for them, helping them to understand the unspoken rules that impact these spaces, develop strategies to get past these barriers, and build a career that maximizes their potential and helps them realize their dreams.

A recognized expert on DEI and a range of workplace issues, organizational psychologist Ella F. Washington, PhD, is the founder and CEO of Ellavate Solutions, an integrated DEI strategy firm, and the author of *The Necessary Journey: Making Real Progress on Equity and Inclusion*. She is a professor of practice at Georgetown University's McDonough School of Business, where she has won honors, including Excellence in Teaching 2021 and Poet and Quants 40 under 40 MBA Professors in 2023. Additionally, she is the founder of the Ellavate Charity Foundation and a sought-after author, speaker, and consultant. Prior to founding Ellavate, Dr. Washington led Gallup's Diversity and Inclusion practice and served as the cohost of Gallup's Center of Black Voices Cultural Competence Podcast. She lives in Washington, DC.

INTRODUCTION

My mother often complained about her job.

It wasn't that she hated it because being a nurse had always been her childhood dream. Ever since she was burned in a fire at the age of four and had skin grafts as part of her treatment, she was fascinated with the way the nurses at the hospital cared for her. This sparked something inside, and she knew from that moment that nursing would be her career path. She pursued it passionately and was a nurse from the start of her career until retirement. She loved the work of nursing. Yet, at times, she hated her job.

She hated being treated differently than some of her colleagues. She hated how the goalposts for measuring her performance kept moving. Today, we would call these "workplace stressors" or "microaggressions," but back then, we didn't have specific terminology beyond some version of "my job sucks." Even though my mother loved her work, aspects of her job *did* suck, not because of her patients or even the bureaucratic system she had to deal with, but because the *human* side of her work environment was failing her.

This conflict still holds true for many working people today. Even when we're blessed to be doing work we're passionate about, many of us are like my mom. We work in environments that do not set us up for success or create the conditions that enable us to thrive.

My mission is to fix this. I want to make the workplace better for people like me, people like my mom, and anyone who has been marginalized in any way. The fact is most of us have to work for a living. And because we spend a solid third of our lives doing that work, I'm taking the radical position that work does *not* have to break our souls. At this moment, unfortunately, the data paints a different picture. According to Gallup's 2023 State of the Workplace Report:

- 77 percent of employees are unhappy (meaning not engaged or actively disengaged) at work,

- 51 percent of currently employed workers state that they are watching for or actively seeking a new job,

- 44 percent of global employees report experiencing significant daily stress, and

- 52 percent of employees in the United States and Canada report being worried, sad, and/or angry at work.[1]

So many of us go through life automatically assuming that work will always be hard and stressful, and will always suck. We assume we will never find happiness within the confines of our job. And when we assume work is oppressive, we sometimes feed into the narrative that creates that oppression. Unfortunately, that assumption does apply to some work environments, but I think most of them can deliver a better experience for all of us if we change the dynamics of the workplace and maybe even our expectations. Bringing that kind of progress to our working lives became my mission when I started this career almost twenty years ago. It's also why I wrote this book.

Before we go any further, allow me to introduce myself.

I'm Dr. Ella F. Washington, an organizational psychologist who operates at the intersection of business, diversity, and leadership. My mission is to *elevate humanity in the workplace*. I'm the founder and CEO of DEI (diversity, equity, and inclusion) consulting firm Ellavate Solutions and a professor of practice at Georgetown University's McDonough School of Business. I'm also the author of *The Necessary Journey: Making Real Progress on Equity and Inclusion*.

Throughout my career exploring the psychology of the corporate world, I have consistently noticed this pervasive sense of *IYKYK* (*if you know, you know*). I often felt left out in certain situations, like not being invited to meetings or missing out on important communication that others seemed to receive. It was even more frustrating when I realized that those who didn't fit in the typical mold were the ones experiencing these moments more often. I wanted to ask if I was missing something or if there were certain rules I should be aware of.

I wrote this book to help people feel seen and know that they are not crazy; there *are* unspoken rules to the corporate world. And, most importantly, I wrote it to help demystify some of these rules through the tactics I provide. I come to you with nearly twenty years of experience helping shape a fairer, more equitable, and ultimately more successful workplace, so I understand the experience of those who have been marginalized. In addition, I conducted over one hundred hours of interviews with people from all walks of life to gather their experiences facing and dealing with these unspoken rules. Finally, I bring my own lived experience to this book, moments I thought I might never share publicly, hoping that others might see part of themselves in me and gain some insight or inspiration for their own journey.

This book is not specifically a "DEI book," but rather, this is a *knowledge* book. Whether or not your workplace was made with people like you or me in mind, most of us enter the corporate world with some gaps in the IYKYK arena. But that does not mean success in these spaces is not possible. IYKYK holds less value as an exclusionary practice when you do know. Knowledge is power, and applied knowledge is liberation from systems of exclusion.[2]

Creating a Better Workplace

My first book, *The Necessary Journey*, was very much a DEI book. I wrote it in the wake of George Floyd's murder, as a guide to help corporate leaders, fresh off the slew of corporate pledges to DEI initiatives, make real, meaningful changes within their organizations. The response was overwhelmingly positive. However, the pendulum continues to swing back and forth regarding support for DEI, as well as the commitment of budget and resources to its implementation.

As I write this book, there's a lot of political commentary about how "D-E-I must die." People are focused on the acronym instead of the work being done. This has led some practitioners to shy away from the term or the words used in the term and try to turn the conversation to what they are actually doing—which is trying to increase representation and respect for everyone. And that work, whatever you call it, is not new. It's been going on since before the American civil rights movement and will continue to be done, whatever people might choose to call it, regardless of where the political pendulum may swing. It's all part of the continuum of people trying to make this world a more equitable place. I have no idea what we'll be calling this work in ten years, but I know the work will still be being done.

Meanwhile, I continue to hear from *The Necessary Journey* readers sharing their personal struggles to find their sense of place and purpose in corporate spaces. They're asking questions like the following: *What about me? How do I make sense of and navigate my workplace? How do I show up authentically when I'm the only person who looks like me? Do I even belong here? Is it OK to negotiate for more? Is this all in my head?*

To be honest, most people experience this kind of uncertainty in the workplace at one time or another. It's not like there's a "playbook" for corporate spaces. Well, actually, there is, but it was written long ago for a very specific group of people—white, cisgender men. People with nondominant identities[3] (meaning everyone else), based on factors like race and gender, which is the work I know best, as well as socioeconomic status, sexuality, ability, neurodiversity, and more, typically lack access to this playbook. Even a cisgender white man who's, say, a first-generation student, or first generation in the corporate world, may not have anyone in their life who can help them understand the unspoken rules that govern these spaces.

For example, my parents both had graduate degrees. My mother was a nurse, and my father was an engineer. He had a long career in the military, which gave him some degree of experience navigating workplace politics. Working his way up to become a colonel as a Black man was a big deal at the time. But there was still only so much he could offer me in terms of understanding the unspoken rules of the corporate world. As for my mother, most of these rules didn't show up in nursing. They also didn't show up in education, where I started, and where I now work (although there are unspoken rules in academia, too, just different ones).

Keep in mind, I'm not talking about those basic rules everyone should be aware of going into any workplace, which include:

- show up to work on time,

---

3   In society, everyone is assigned multiple social identity groups. Within each category, there is a social status and hierarchy with dominant and nondominant identities. Historically, dominant cultural identities have had more influence and resources and granted privileges, while people from nondominant groups have had lesser resources and have often been systematically disadvantaged (racism, sexism, heterosexism, ableism, etc.).

- do what you say you're going to do,

- act with integrity,

- respect the people around you, and

- take ownership of the work that you do.

Those things are your responsibility. It's also your responsibility to learn your organization's culture, which you will learn largely through experience. This book is not intended to be a substitute for any of that. It *can't* be. However, especially if you're from a nondominant identity, there are likely to be some gaps between the rules you know and the rules you don't know, especially when it comes to developing power and influence in your workplace.

If you google the term "power and influence" right now, the number one book that would likely come up is *The 48 Laws of Power* by Robert Greene. The book is popular because it has a lot of useful advice. However, many of Greene's tips, even things I consider good advice, fail to take identity into account. It's power and influence but through a white, cisgender, male lens. When it comes to anyone else, many of those "laws" don't apply.

For example, one of Greene's tips is to "be aggressive and take no prisoners." Well, if you happen to be a Black man, there is already a stereotype of you being aggressive.[4] And, while it's *only* a stereotype, research has shown that it has actual consequences in certain contexts. Inasmuch as Black men are commonly stereotyped as frightening, scary, and menacing, Black men in mostly white environments find themselves managing this image to minimize its resonance with white peers. Thus, they may face pressure to avoid behaving in ways that reflect this stereotype. So, being aggressive and taking no prisoners is not going to work the same way for a Black man.[5]

Similarly, if you're a Black female, there is also an "angry Black woman" stereotype you need to contend with.[6,7] My previous research has explored these stereotypes and penalties against Black female leaders.[8] There are also stereotypes around anger if you are a woman in general. Research on gender, anger expression, and status revealed that in a professional setting, men who showed anger were seen as having higher status compared to men who showed sadness. Interestingly, both male and female evaluators tended to give lower status to angry female professionals compared to angry male professionals.[9]

Beyond the issue of anger, research is quite clear that the perceptions and expectations of individuals in the workplace have a lot to do with their identity.[10] From research on the assumptions of competence, shifting performance standards, backlash for acting counter to stereotypes,[11] and situational power,[12] there are decades of research findings in organizational behavior literature that demonstrate identity plays a role in how people experience the workplace. People from nondominant identities need an enlightened set of strategies to grow their power and influence in corporate spaces.

That's what this book's "cheat codes" are all about. They're designed to speed up the learning curve and reveal these unspoken rules so that you don't have to spend years and years figuring them out.

To be clear, you will still have your own experiences—but hopefully, if we can plant the right seeds now through the information provided in this book, those hidden "rules of the road" will be visible earlier, and you will get up to speed in dealing with them effectively more quickly. The universal cheat codes in this book will help you navigate these spaces successfully as *who you are* and develop power and influence skills to be successful.

No matter where you are in your career and life, you may eventually find yourself in a space where you feel unseen. And you need the right tools to take control of the situation. If your company isn't providing them, this book will and will help you get to where you want to go through your own power. If you're blessed to work for a company that *is* providing them, this book will help you maximize those opportunities.

The Unspoken Rules

Who comes into the workplace knowing these unspoken rules? Typically, it's people who have been exposed to the language of business from an early age—generally, people who have parents or close family members in those kinds of circles. Then, again, we can't make assumptions. I had a student in my undergraduate class, a junior in business school for years, tell me he didn't know what "IB" meant. As a first-generation American from a Southeast Asian background, no one he knew growing up had ever talked about investment banking. Exposure only comes from experience, especially early on. You can get that exposure once you're into your career, but gaining it prior to that can be enormously helpful.

There are other ways to learn these unspoken rules, such as mentorship and, eventually, sponsorship. However, not all mentorships are equal. If you don't have a mentor who has navigated the same or similar experiences to what you are going through, or one who is willing to be honest about how identity plays a role in these experiences, they may not be able to help much when it comes to grasping the unspoken rules. Half of the battle is finding a mentor who's had a lived experience of navigating identity in the workplace.[13]

The second half of the battle is that person must be willing to share those cheat codes with you. Not everyone is. The famous 1973 "Queen Bee Phenomenon"[14] provided a theory explaining women's reluctance to help other women. This theory pertains to a woman in a position of power who is more critical of female subordinates than male subordinates. Over fifty years later, studies show the phenomenon still exists,[15] characterizing the "queen bee" as a woman who rises to a top management position and then behaves in a way that is unhelpful or even purposely thwarts the efforts of other women to advance their careers.[16]

Even when they don't rise (or sink) to the level of actual sabotage, for a certain type of woman, the extent of their "mentoring" might be to say, "I made it so you can make it too. Why are you complaining about being a woman?" as opposed to "Here's how I handled it. This might work for you." Black or Latin people may say, "You need to just work harder," as opposed to, "I'm going to help you through this because I experienced it." This kind of ritualized suffering for newbies is called hazing, and it's still very much a thing in corporate America, depending on the organization.[17] If your work environment encourages hazing, "mentorship" may amount to advice like, "I had to stay up all night and do all these annoying things, so you do too." They don't give their mentees the real talk, the download, the information—the things you definitely won't find in the HR handbook.

Why I Wrote This Book

Ultimately, I wrote this book for anyone who has ever felt lost in the workplace, especially if that feeling limits their power, influence, and ability to grow the career they want. Even white, cisgender, heterosexual men can feel lost in corporate spaces—especially now, in a world where cancel culture is rampant, and they may feel threatened by the workplace evolution and feelings of *Where do I fit in?* (Not that they should feel this way, as these spaces and the rules that govern them were largely designed for them. However, they may.[18])

I wrote it for every professional who's asked these questions, who's battled imposter syndrome and systemic exclusion, who's wondered how to expand their power and influence and even whether it's OK to do so. It's really for anyone looking for a way to make work suck less.

We all need support and skills in navigating an ever-changing corporate landscape, especially now. And while this book is not intended to be a "leadership book," leaders need these skills too. As we all work toward more inclusive workspaces where everyone's contributions are welcomed, valued, and celebrated, my hope is that these skills become as universal as possible so that they can be applied not just on a national but also on a global scale. Living in a global economy means more moments of connection between people from different cultures and countries. The skills I will teach in this book are, ultimately, universal because they are all about accessing and operating as your authentic self.

We will explore the unspoken rules that determine success in corporate settings, coaching you in the tactics that will empower you to shape a successful career anchored in meaningful experiences. I'll share practical strategies you can use to own your story and build your strengths, leverage your skills, and identify opportunities to excel and advance. You'll learn from the experiences of others who've success-fully navigated these spaces, explore fascinating research, and build your capacity to move forward more confidently.

My intention is for you to walk away with everything you need to uncover and manage the unspoken rules in any workplace, even those that may be uncomfortable, unfamiliar, or where you may be "the only one." You'll learn you're not paranoid or crazy when you run into invisible walls, and you'll be able to use this book's practical, actionable content to overcome them, allowing you to thrive in corporate environments, develop leadership skills, and achieve your career goals. You'll also discover how to negotiate from a position of power, building your situational awareness and your capacity for effective, results-oriented action. Finally, you'll be able to identify the conversations and experiences that will deliver opportunities for excellence.

This is especially important for professionals from nondominant identities as the political pendulum continues to swing. In 2020, after the George Floyd murder, $66 billion[19] were committed to social justice and DEI. As I write this book, in 2024, things appear to be shifting. There is a gap between public sentiment and what the data shows. Some reports say companies are not pulling back, while others say the opposite. Verbally, organizations may be saying, "We still have the same values and mission, and we're still committed," but they may not be putting money or internal resources behind that commitment. What is clear is that there has been a shift in the fervor and explicit support for DEI that we saw in 2020. For example:

- In 2023, attrition rates for DEI roles outpaced those of non-DEI roles at more than six hundred US companies that laid off workers.[20]

- SCOTUS 2023 ruling on affirmative action has increased the attention and polarization of DEI topics, with some employers pulling back from their efforts.[21]

- More than thirty bills have been introduced across the United States to ban DEI. Some have passed in states including Florida, Tennessee, North Dakota, North Carolina, Texas, and Oklahoma.[22]

At the same time, according to a 2023 Pew Research study,[23] most US workers say focusing on DEI at work is a good thing, but a relatively small share places great importance on diversity in their workplace. Overall, opinions about DEI vary considerably along demographic and political lines. Meanwhile, the workplace demographics will continue to become more diverse in the United States[24] and globally[25]—generationally, racially, and regarding gender identity.[26] Wherever your organization might stand on the DEI issues at a given moment in time, this book is designed to give you the tools to advance your career, whoever you are.

How to Use This Book

My previous book, *The Necessary Journey*, explored strategies that leading global organizations were implementing to achieve progress in equity and inclusion. This book aims to continue the ongoing discussion on valuable knowledge, insights, and means to achieve success. It will not only benefit the readers but also provide resources for corporate teams and employee resource groups (ERGs) to retain and develop future leaders more effectively.

SECTION ONE

Developing your playbook starts with self awareness.

Look internally to understand who you are, both in the workplace and as a human being.

SECTION TWO

How are you showing up in the workplace right now?

Examine the ways you experience and navigate your current space with others.

SECTION THREE

Look forward by moving beyond what's right in front of you.

Develop your own playbook to build a career and a life that fits and nourishes the person you are.

The book is divided into three main sections. The first three chapters will help you look internally to understand who you are, both in the workplace and as a human being. The second three chapters will focus on how you are showing up in the workplace and strategies to make the most of your experience there. The book's final part will look forward by helping you move beyond what's right in front of you and thinking outside the box to build a career and a life that fits and nourishes the person you are. In each chapter, I'll call your attention to the unspoken rules that govern that particular area, along with strategies, or "cheat codes," to help you tackle challenges and come out ahead.

Think of this book as your guide through your own necessary journey. I hope you feel seen and see yourself represented in ways that maybe you've never seen yourself represented before. And I hope you ultimately understand that you do belong, that there's a place for you, and it's not a place where you must accept whatever you're given or twist yourself into a pretzel shape to fit in. The stories and strategies I share in this book are designed for professionals of different identities, fields, and stages of their careers because I believe everyone deserves a circle of inclusion and influence.

Part of the cheat code is understanding that, unless you are a white, cisgender, heterosexual male, the corporate environment was likely not made for you (and if you are, you may face other issues of belonging). You can decide to do something else, like entrepreneurship, which has its own barriers. Or you can say, "OK, I want to be in this corporate space because I'm passionate about this job. I like the company," or whatever your reason is, "And I'm going to navigate it against all odds, even though it's not made for me." Of course, the organization must do their part to change some of these structural barriers. But this book is about the things *you* can do and control to navigate your own path.

My hope is that this book will provide guidance and motivation, no matter who you are or where you are working because we all deserve that opportunity. And make no mistake, it benefits all of humanity when that opportunity is available for all. As Martin Luther King Jr. famously said, "Whatever affects one directly, affects all indirectly." This is an effort to unlock everyone's potential. I hope it makes whatever work you do a better, more rewarding experience.

SCAN ME

A S S E S S M E N T

How Strong Is Your Career Playbook?

Before you dive into creating your own playbook, take this assessment so you can evaluate when you're starting.

You can also take this live at **https://ellafwashington.com/ assessment/** for a full analysis of your responses.

1. I know how to navigate the unspoken or unwritten rules for career advancement in my workplace.

    □ Strongly Agree

    □ Agree

    □ Neutral

    □ Disagree

    □ Strongly Disagree

2. When someone asks me to tell them about myself, my answer is brief, relatable, and memorable.

    □ Strongly Agree

    □ Agree

□ Neutral

□ Disagree

□ Strongly Disagree

3. I can articulate my unique strengths at work.

□ Strongly Agree

□ Agree

□ Neutral

□ Disagree

□ Strongly Disagree

4. I hold myself to a personal standard of excellence that applies to everything I seek to accomplish.

□ Strongly Agree

□ Agree

□ Neutral

□ Disagree

□ Strongly Disagree

5. I use the same standard of excellence at work as I do at home and in other areas of my life.

□ Strongly Agree

□ Agree

□ Neutral

□ Disagree

□ Strongly Disagree

6. During negotiations, I understand how to align my expectations with those of others to achieve my goals.

☐ Strongly Agree

☐ Agree

☐ Neutral

☐ Disagree

☐ Strongly Disagree

7. Mentors and other trusted advisors help guide my career-based decisions.

☐ Strongly Agree

☐ Agree

☐ Neutral

☐ Disagree

☐ Strongly Disagree

8. I can clearly describe my desired career path over the next five years.

☐ Strongly Agree

☐ Agree

☐ Neutral

☐ Disagree

☐ Strongly Disagree

9. I feel confident in my ability to navigate power dynamics in my workplace.

□ Strongly Agree

□ Agree

□ Neutral

□ Disagree

□ Strongly Disagree

10. I regularly attend classes, workshops, and other formal learning opportunities to support my career growth.

□ Strongly Agree

□ Agree

□ Neutral

□ Disagree

□ Strongly Disagree

11. I add unique value to my organization using my talents and passion.

□ Strongly Agree

□ Agree

□ Neutral

□ Disagree

□ Strongly Disagree

12. My professional priorities are aligned with my personal priorities over the next five years.

- □ Strongly Agree
- □ Agree
- □ Neutral
- □ Disagree
- □ Strongly Disagree

13. I have the skills to influence others to support my goals at work.

- □ Strongly Agree
- □ Agree
- □ Neutral
- □ Disagree
- □ Strongly Disagree

SECTION ONE

Developing your playbook starts with self awareness.

Look internally to understand who you are, both in the workplace and as a human being.

SECTION ONE

CHAPTER ONE

Own Your Story

To know thyself is the beginning of wisdom.

—SOCRATES

I had a client who felt like he didn't belong in his workplace—a workplace that happened to be a finance company in Boston. This wasn't because of his skills on the job or even where he went to school. It was because of *vacations*. Every Monday all summer long, this client's coworkers would come back to the office filled with stories about what they did that weekend on Nantucket, which, for those who don't know, is an island off Massachusetts frequented by the well-to-do. It felt like almost everyone in this workplace "vacationed" on Nantucket. Everyone but my client. He had never even used "vacation" as a verb.

His frequent traveling colleagues had no idea they were causing my client any discomfort. Because they all worked together at the same firm and were in the same socioeconomic cohort, they assumed he knew exactly what they were talking about when they reminisced about who they bumped into and where they ate. They didn't know my client had never been to Nantucket because he didn't come from a background where anyone in his family would ever go to a place like that for just a weekend.

They didn't know because my client didn't tell them. He never felt comfortable saying, "I've never been there before" or "Tell me about it." He didn't want to call attention to this thing that made him different.

This sort of thing happens in workplaces all the time. There's an aspect of the culture that's significant but that some people feel is not *for them.* The same thing happens with golf. For decades, a certain type of business has been done on the golf course. But not everyone plays golf. And not everyone feels comfortable saying, "Not only do I not know how to play golf, but I actually prefer to play basketball on the weekend." Especially if they happen to be a Black male.

That discomfort is what you feel when you're breaking an unspoken rule. If the unspoken rule is that everybody plays golf, or the unspoken rule is that we all go to Nantucket, and you don't, you feel different. You feel "other."

🔒 UNSPOKEN RULE:

Who you are *outside* of work impacts who you are *inside* of work.

So, what are you supposed to do about it?

As with most things in life, you have a few choices. You can learn to play golf, especially if the deals are conducted on the golf course. But areas like this, where your story differs from most of your peers, are also opportunities to get comfortable sharing some of the things that make you *you.* In order to be able to do that, you have to *own your story.*

I vividly remember my AP history class in high school. It was my favorite class, and why wouldn't it be? I loved history, and I was good at it. I might have become a historian if I hadn't become a psychologist (my second favorite AP class). But that's not the only reason I remember AP history so well. That class, the one I loved, was, unfortunately, one of the first places I remember the experience of feeling "othered"—being made to feel different in a negative way.

I grew up in the South, in Durham, North Carolina, where I attended a high school that was evenly mixed between Black and white students. When I was younger, the schools had been redistricted, which sparked many protests—because the white people didn't want their kids to go to the historically Black high school. They all wanted their children to go to the traditionally white, nationally ranked public high school, which also happened to be my high school. Thanks to that redistricting, the school was split about fifty-fifty along racial lines—with one major exception. In my AP classes, which, in my case, made up most of my core classes, it looked like redistricting never happened. I was either the only Black student in the room or one of only two or three.

I lived a dual existence. In the AP classes, I had almost a different personality to match the room's population. Then, when the bell rang, and I went out into the hallway to get to my next class, I saw all my friends and felt more relaxed and like, well, like me. In other words, I became a master at "code-switching,"[27] even though I had no idea I was doing it—let alone what code-switching was. In class, I never talked about being Black, even though I was visibly Black, and everyone could see my Blackness. Then again, when people talked about their experiences, I never talked about my parents being divorced or anything that was genuinely personal. Like a lot of people of color, I grew up feeling that school, and by extension the workplace, was for *other people*. And you just don't air your dirty laundry in a place that's not for you.

I felt this way despite the fact I did well in high school. I got all A's and graduated as one of the top students in my class. I was both student body president and homecoming queen. I was well respected, well liked, and well adjusted. But sitting in those AP classes, I still felt like I was inhabiting a space that was "not for me." I also had no inkling that there was anything abnormal or wrong about feeling that way. I just accepted it as the way things were. What I didn't realize was that, inside those classrooms, I was cutting off part of my humanity. Not that I expected anyone to create the kind of space that would tell me I was welcome as is. It was just not a thing.

So, when my AP history class was discussing the very real Black experiences of slavery and the civil rights movement, the class, teacher included, looked to me to share my experiences because I was one of the few Black students there. The teacher never explicitly asked me to share my experiences; it was more of a vibe. When we were discussing the horrors of slavery or discrimination, I could feel everyone's eyes on me, like I was the designated ambassador of Black pain. To this day, I still don't know exactly what they expected me to say or do.

Eventually, once our grades started coming in and everyone realized I was smart enough to be there, some of my classmates aligned with me. They made me feel safe and not othered. They treated me like one of them, a fellow college-bound student dealing with the massive workload of AP classes. But this certainly wasn't my experience with everyone. For every white classmate I remember connecting with, there were many who made me feel different, even unintentionally—a group that, unfortunately, included many of my teachers.

That's why, when I thought about college, I wanted to be in a space where I would feel more comfortable and accepted. While I lived less than fifteen minutes from the University of North Carolina (UNC)—Chapel Hill and Duke University, two of the best schools in the country, I did not choose either of those institutions, even though I could have gone to UNC for free and would have gotten a full ride to Duke. I wanted to be in a place where I felt seen, and to me, the perfect choice was Spelman College, an all-female historically black college and university (HBCU) in Atlanta, Georgia.

Visiting Spelman for the first time was like being in one of those cartoons where someone walks into a room and, suddenly, everything lights up. I was overcome with this feeling of belonging. *This is for me*, I thought. Not just me as a woman, not just me as a Black person, but also me as a Black woman with all of my complexities, humanity, and individuality. That was the other aspect of Spelman I vividly remember. They make it clear when you visited the campus that you could get a good education anywhere, but only at this institution could you be developed as a whole person.

Ironically, Spelman is where I first became interested in studying diversity. You would assume that because the Black, female students were homogeneous demographically, we didn't have to have diversity conversations. But that's far from the truth. We didn't have to focus on the things that usually stop the conversation, race and gender, so we were free to dive into deeper issues like gender identity, sexuality, ability, socioeconomic status, colorism, and so many other topics that were unusual to discuss back then but are now commonplace in our culture.

I also learned that groups of humans will always have an in-group and out-group experience, what psychologists call "social identity theory."[28] You can look globally to places that don't have a lot of racial differences, but you will undoubtedly find they have caste systems, tribal identities, and/or economic differences that they use to in-group and out-group people. In other words, even if we were all, say, the same shade of green, we'd still find ways to declare some people "like us" and others as, well, "other." To discover that was the typical human experience was fascinating to me. To be sure, Spelman has meant many things to me in terms of my career and my values, but one specific, maybe surprising by-product of attending this all-Black, all-female institution is this: I was now able to see diversity in a much broader and deeper way than just race and gender.

Then, I went to Northwestern University for graduate school and experienced whiplash. The "othering" I endured there was probably even worse than what I had gone through in high school because, in high school, I still had the sense of community and safety of my family and friends I'd known since elementary school. But now I was living in Chicago, the furthest I'd ever lived from home, and I felt like I spent the entire four years disguising who I was in many ways. Once again, I felt like I could not be my authentic self. Yes, I loved what I was studying, but I hated the overall experience. I was the only Black person in my cohort. Northwestern was known for having Black scholars, and I did have Black people in the program ahead of me. But in my everyday classrooms, once again, I was the only Black person, and I constantly felt othered. I was also pursuing a different path than my fellow students, who all wanted to stay in the ivory tower and teach. I wanted to be out there in the business world, making a difference, further alienating me from everyone else.

It was like what my mother always said about being a nurse—that she loved her work but hated the job. When I talked with her about how miserable I was in grad school, I found out just how similar we were. My mother revealed that she went through the same thing I was going through in her master's program, which was why she didn't go for her PhD. Twenty-some years later, not enough had changed because I still felt like I had no resources to help me navigate this kind of experience. The truth is, while many people think I got my PhD in just four years, at the age of twenty-five, because I'm some genius, the reality is that I did it because I just wanted to get out of there. I just wanted to get out into the world and start making things better.

That was my story before entering the workplace. This chapter, which starts your journey, will help you discover *your* story, which, in turn, will put you in the best possible position for success. So, let's look inward, discover who you truly are, and own the story that brought you to where you are today.

The Story of You

There are numerous books available that teach us how to "know ourselves" and help us in various ways to achieve that goal. However, the purpose of this book is not to guide you on that path. Instead, this chapter aims to assist you in owning your story, which means comprehending your life's journey so far. Your "narrative identity" is essentially your life story, as described in psychology. In other words, this chapter is designed to help you understand and take control of your narrative. In technical terms, "Narrative identity is a person's internalized and evolving life story, integrating the reconstructed past and imagined future to provide life with some degree of unity and purpose. Through narrative identity, people convey to themselves and to others who they are now, how they came to be, and where they think their lives may be going in the future."[29]

Your narrative identity includes all the experiences, events, relationships, and choices that got you where you are today. Knowing your story means developing self-awareness, by understanding how your mind works and how your thoughts and emotions influence your actions, as well as your core beliefs and values. It's understanding what makes you tick. When you truly own your story, you understand how these various threads have combined to make you the uniquely capable human that you are.

Owning your story is especially beneficial for people with multicultural identities. One study found that people with multicultural identities who had "narrative coherence" had a higher sense of well-being.[30] However, I believe it's crucial for anyone embarking on this journey to own their story because it's the only way to fully grasp how and why you move through the world with your unique vantage point.

I developed my story through introspection and analysis, growing to understand more about who I was, what I had been through, and what it said about me and the social institutions that govern us. That process took me some time, and I only got there through therapy, life, and loss. Before that, I used to take my family background for granted. I didn't see how it impacted my identity. But I realized that many of the values I bring to the workplace were instilled in me at home as a young girl. My mother always told me, "Do your best," but she never measured my performance against anyone else, and she didn't judge me if I didn't perform well. I understood that she truly expected me to do *my* best, which created the standard of excellence for me. I knew when I was not giving my all, and that was more sobering than her being upset with me for a bad grade. When I did struggle, she would try to find positive solutions to help me do better—for example, hiring a tutor when I needed extra help with a subject. Now, whether I'm identifying and solving problems in the workplace or helping my students understand a complex issue, those values come into play.

On the contrary, my Southern upbringing emphasized showing respect over authenticity—which is why I had trouble addressing my grad school professors by their first names, even though that was the norm at that level and necessary for me to be taken seriously as a scholar. That was a mental obstacle I had to overcome. But I wouldn't have known it was an obstacle if I hadn't taken the time to understand where I come from and why I did the things I did.

Jessica Lin, director in finance, has a similar experience:

When I started working, I don't think I really ever thought about identity at all. I kind of was just like, "I'm just like everyone else. I'm here to do a job." I've been working over ten years, and I've realized how much of the way I think and operate has been driven from my parents and a very traditional Asian perspective, versus what I've needed to do to be successful at work. I think that has been my identity journey at work. I've had really good support systems from predominantly white male leaders who have brought me along the way, but I've had to learn a lot about my instincts. For example, I was taught in my family, "You just do your work, you do the best at your work, you don't say anything, just get your work done." When I was in consulting, so much of what you needed to do was talk about yourself and talk about "Here's all the great things that I did. Here's how quickly I did them." Frankly, I still struggle with talking about myself sometimes. I recently had the thought, "Isn't it kind of sad that I want people to just see me as a good employee and I don't want anyone to know more about my background?"

Owning your story means looking at your entire background, including:

- where you're from,

- who your parents were,

- what they taught you (either by example or by explanation),

- what made you feel bad,

- what made you feel good,

- where you succeeded,

- where you failed, and

- whatever else you deem relevant to your identity today.

In other words, your story encompasses your entire history, a history you may not have given much thought to or contextualized in any way. This is where the second aspect of owning your story—discussing it with people from different backgrounds than yourself—comes in. It's only through engaging with people who are *not* like you that you begin to see and understand all the things that make you unique.

For example, when talking to people who grew up in Durham, North Carolina, I find we all have similar backgrounds and experiences. It wasn't until I got to college that I finally encountered people who didn't grow up like me on a regular basis. When I got into the workplace, I noticed even more things that made me different from my colleagues. And I realized that no matter what your background is, talking with people, being in community with people, learning about people who had different upbringings, opens your eyes to why you do the things you do. It's hard to see that information if you're just in your little bubble, whether it's your personal bubble or the bubble of people who've known you since you were two, including your family.

Gaining that broader perspective helps you gain the following abilities:

- You understand more about other kinds of people.

- You understand more about yourself.

- You can better grasp the dynamics of creating positive relationships with those different from you.

- You're more equipped to avoid conflicts and clashes with others and deal with them when it's unavoidable.

All of these combine to create a personal skill set that will help you navigate your career positively and productively. However, when you don't own your story, it can have the opposite impact on your well-being. As Jessica Lin remembers,

I moved to the States in first grade, and I have distinct memories of wanting to fit in at my predominantly white schools. I hated sandwiches, but I forced my parents to make me sandwiches every day for lunch so I could fit in. I threw out the sandwiches each day, but this was better than being mocked for bringing traditional Asian food. Throughout high school and college, I assumed I was like everyone else, and it never occurred to me that I had this very specific identity. Going to work as an adult was the first time I realized how much I am like my mom—I don't boast about anything, I don't give myself a pat on the back, and I don't speak up. This was the first time I realized how important my identity was. It took me a really long time to grapple with that and understand that identity influenced how I showed up at work.

Three Identities, Three Ways of "Showing Up"

Let's say you manage to get to a place where you do understand your own story and you own it. This helps you achieve what's called "identity integration," which is "the process of bringing together various aspects of one's self into a coherent whole, and the sense of self-continuity and wholeness that emerges as a result of these processes."[31] Achieving this state means you don't feel compelled to pretend to be someone you're not—and you don't lose your sense of self. Inside, you know yourself, and believe me, that's a great gift.

The next thing to consider is how you show up in any given situation. This can be hard to do on your own, because, despite what I just said about developing an integrated identity, you still will end up having not one single identity, but three of them. The following represent those three "faces" of you, or your self-concept as defined by psychologist Carl Rogers:[32]

1. How you see yourself

2. How others see you

3. How you want to see yourself in the future (Ideal self)

Let's look at them in turn. First, how you see yourself represents how well you understand your story. Internally, you know who you are and what your values are. You carry that with you wherever you go. However, your self-esteem, which is a combination of how others see you and how you think you compare to them, may be an entirely different one. Depending on how you present yourself to others, you may be unaware of the disconnect between who you know you are and who they think you are. The third facet of your self-concept is how you want to see yourself in the future—in other words, your aspirational self.

Whether you know it or not, you are constantly assessing your competence and character and shaping others' perceptions. That work of bringing the way you believe people see you in line with the way you want them to see you (your aspirational self) is called "professional image construction."[33]

When you communicate the person you aspire to be, others are aware of your goals and ambitions and may be sympathetic to helping you progress in that direction. However, if they don't know you have your eye on a specific prize, you can hardly expect them to telepathically pick up on your ambitions. At times, you have to grapple with how you are showing up, which is not aligned with your aspirational self.

I remember being at a birthday party some years ago, sharing that I was stressed at work, and a college friend kindly but honestly said, "Ella, you are always stressed; it's kind of your mode of operation." At that moment, I was floored, not because she was wrong but because she was right. I desired to be seen as well prepared, organized, and well balanced. I vividly remember my first boss, who was always frazzled, rushing from meetings to meetings, and had no time to make real human connections. I vowed at twenty-two that I never wanted to show up like that at work, yet here I was a decade later, being told that was almost exactly how I was showing up, not just at work but in my personal life as well. Though I was hurt in the moment, I was immensely grateful for that friend's candid feedback. I realized my behaviors had to match the image of how I saw myself and wanted to be perceived by others.

This brings us to the following truth: because we do have these three aspects to our self-concept, there is often a huge gap between our self-image (how we see ourselves) and how others perceive us. For example, if you're smart but hold back on expressing that intelligence around others, they may have no idea of your intellectual capability. How accurately people "get" you is all a function of how you show up. Many of us neglect to focus on how we show up, which means we're easily misunderstood and even misjudged.

Obviously, you can't understand how you're coming off to people on your own. The best way to find out is to ask others questions like the following:

- What do you enjoy most about working with me?

- What do you see as the biggest area in which I need to improve?

- From your perspective, what is something I care deeply about in life?

- Name one character trait I could work to improve upon.[34]

- What could I do or stop doing that would make it easier to work with me?[35]

- What are three words you would use to describe me?

- What are three words you would use to describe how I show up at work?

- When do you notice I am at my best?

It's not easy to quiz other people like this, especially if you're coworkers without a real relationship outside the office. So let them know in advance that you are working on your personal brand and would like their honest feedback on how you show up at work. However, if you want to have a better experience wherever you work, it's a muscle you'll want to start exercising so that you can get comfortable with it. To be clear, I'm not asking you to march into work tomorrow and start interrogating random people about their impressions of you. My advice is to begin trying this with people you already feel comfortable with and know well, even your friends, and work your way up.

When you understand how you're showing up and compare who people think you are with the person you know you are, you can make the kinds of adjustments that will allow you to be more authentic in the workplace and be more genuine with others. You can also look more critically at how you fit into the environment in which you will be operating. You can acknowledge areas of discomfort and disconnection and act to navigate whatever space you're in more confidently.

When I started my career, I wasn't showing up as the person I wanted to be. I struggled to balance showing respect, which was part of my Southern cultural roots, and being authentic. Of course, I wanted to do my best; that was always my mindset. But I also wanted someone to tell me what my next step should be. That hesitance to carve out my path made others think I lacked initiative and creativity. Once I knew my story and decoded the unwritten rules that shaped the space I was in, I realized it was OK to think and create solutions outside the box. That, in turn, showed others I was more than they thought I was. In this way, I was also finally showing my aspirational self, the person I wanted to become—someone comfortable with finding new, innovative answers to organizational problems.

Understanding and sometimes adjusting your self-concept enable you to determine a way forward that honors who you are and who you want to become. What that looks like probably depends on who you are and where you are. Because even today, in many work environments from business[36] to medicine[37] to law,[38] how professionalism is defined is based on Cisheteronormative Whiteness—that is, in many professions, on the archetype of the white, cisgender male.

There have been times in my career where I've felt like my merit is what people should be thinking about. But, as we've seen, people don't necessarily think the things about you that you want them to. The reality is that people experience *all* of me, not just whatever my abilities are. When I walk into the room, my PhD is not the only thing they see or hear. They see me as a Black woman, they see me however I'm dressed, they see the color of my usually decorated nails, and they observe one of the many variations of my hairstyles. It's all of me. And my being comfortable with all of me helps me to show up better and recognize when a statement someone makes regarding me isn't necessarily about who I am. It can be about how they see, for example, women in the workplace, or Black people in the workplace, in general. If they have negative views about things like that, it wouldn't matter if you walked in and were the smartest person in the world.[39] Someone with that kind of biased viewpoint can still dismiss you.

🔒 **UNSPOKEN RULE:**

Owning who you are gives you confidence anywhere you show up.

Knowing your story and understanding your identities don't magically make bias go away, but it can help you feel affirmed. Say all your peers went to Ivy League schools, and you went to a state school. When you notice you're having a different experience than your peers, owning your story will give you some understanding of why your experience is different and that you're not crazy for feeling like it is. After all, these are going to be very different experiences, and being able to acknowledge that frees you in a way. You can focus on finding solutions rather than getting bogged down with bad feelings about yourself. I see this a lot at Georgetown with my students from low-income or first-generation backgrounds. They experience the school very differently than upper- and middle-class kids. Fortunately, there are resources I can direct them to, like programs created for first-generation students, to help make their paths a little easier. I can also share my own experiences with them to help them gain some understanding of their situation.

You are an individual. No one else is like you. Owning your story means you accept your differences as a part of who you are and know that those differences can be strengths because they make you unique. Benjamin Collier II, a senior operations executive at a major corporation, understands this.

My upbringing has given me a level of grit and discipline that many of my peers don't have. My mother is a recovering drug addict, my father was in prison for fifteen years of my life, and my two older sisters sacrificed to raise me. Attending Morehouse College was a culture shock. It was the first time that I had been around Black kids who had both parents in the home. Graduating from Morehouse gave me confidence that I could succeed. But I struggled my first two years at Accenture because 90 percent of the time, I was the only person of color on the team, and I often felt lost in their world. In year three, I gained a mentor who encouraged me to bring my whole self to work. And my whole self is, I'm a Black man. I can't change that, I can't hide that, and I can't be ashamed of that. Once I was confident and comfortable in that, I found my stride in corporate America. I didn't have to assimilate to their lifestyles and who they were. I could really be me.

Today I'm blessed to work at a corporation where I can truly bring my entire self to work. That means my adversities—so if my family is struggling, I can talk about it without fear of backlash or being judged. I can bring my entire identity to the workplace, and it's helped me confidently elevate my career.

Some final thoughts. Owning your story isn't about telling yourself a sob story about how hard it is to be you. That's not very helpful. No, it's about leaning into the human side of what you bring to the workplace. What inspires you? What diversity of thought, experience, or interest are you bringing to the conversation? How are you presenting yourself and showing your best to everyone else?

At the same time, imposter syndrome is a real thing. If you aren't familiar with the term, "imposter syndrome is defined as a person's inner belief that their success has occurred due to pure luck, an external mistake, or just hard work but not their abilities or intelligence."[40] Imposter syndrome is incredibly common, and one in three Americans report experiencing it.[41] However, it's more common among women, people of color, and other nondominant identities.[42] I have experienced imposter syndrome. Navigating the corporate landscape can be especially challenging for people with non-dominant identities because those environments were not created for them. To be clear, imposter syndrome is much more about historical and systemic bias and exclusion than it is about your abilities.[43] Those environments, and not knowing the unspoken rules that govern them, create that situation where a person feels like they must be twice as good to get half as far. So, it isn't shocking that women and people of color experience far greater rates of imposter syndrome.

However, you can acknowledge these feelings without letting them conquer you. If you are experiencing imposter syndrome, know that you're not alone and it can be dealt with. Owning your story is a chance to celebrate all the experiences that add up to make you uniquely you. In the remaining chapters, we'll explore how to take that self-knowledge and parlay it into a better, more rewarding workplace experience.

Things to Remember

(At the end of every chapter, I will share several takeaways that translate the key themes into opportunities for personal reflection and action.)

1. Take the time and try to understand your story. The more you understand yourself, the better you'll be able to navigate your career and interactions with others.

2. Determine the differences between how you see yourself and how others see you. Try to understand why some might be getting the wrong idea about you—and how you might change things up to better show up as who you really are and who you want to become.

3. Understand the experiences you've gone through, both good and bad. What made them negative or positive? What role did you play in making them turn out the way they did? What role did others around you play?

CHAPTER EXERCISE: THE ELEVATOR PITCH

(At the end of every chapter, I'll also offer an exercise or experiment you can use to practice the strategies contained in the material.)

If you haven't heard of an elevator pitch, it's simply a capsule summary of something you can complete during an elevator ride. It's also a great way to get clear on and convey your story. Elevator pitches are short, concise, and meant to get your audience's attention. Generally, you want to keep it under thirty seconds.

I find it helpful to break elevator pitches down into three distinct categories: the professional pitch, the future pitch, and the human pitch. These represent three ways you can "show up" in the workplace.

The *professional pitch* is about getting someone (such as a job interviewer or a company executive) interested in what you can bring to a job. Here's an example:

Hi, I'm Maria Lopez, and I'm a first-year consultant. I'm skilled in addressing organizational and efficiency issues, and I'm ultimately interested in managing an office location. I pride myself on my communication skills and implementing change in the most efficient ways possible.

The *future pitch* should be crafted toward the goal of engaging a mentor or potential employer to advance in your field. This elevator pitch focuses less on what you currently do and more on how you want to grow and develop while emphasizing, say, three things you're good at. Here's an example:

My name's Uche Ibrahim. My strongest talents are in messaging, writing, and public speaking because I love finding ways to engage people and "move the needle" when creating buy-in. I've discovered all that during my eight years in corporate life, and I believe I belong in PR.

Finally, we come to what I call the *human pitch*. It's for when someone asks who you are, even if they're not using those exact words. In this pitch, you want to focus on who you are as a person, what makes you tick, how you got to where you are, and where you want to go. When you own your story, this pitch can help you shine. Here's an example:

I'm Felicia Monroe. I grew up in a military family, so we moved around a lot—which meant I had to learn how to connect with new people in new situations on a constant basis. This has served me well in my consulting business, where I'm always meeting new clients and engaging with workforces I've been hired to help. Now, I want to put my core skills to work for causes I really believe in—and help nonprofits find better ways to do community outreach.

One final note. Even though elevator pitches are short, try to layer your response to any "tell me about yourself" question with "hooks" designed to spark further conversation. For example, when the award-winning entrepreneur and magician Vinh Quang Giang is asked the ubiquitous question, "Where are you from?" he doesn't just tell the asker he's from Australia; he also mentions that Australia is home to more things that can kill you than any other country—something almost guaranteed to keep the conversation going.[44]

Now that you've seen a sample of these three different kinds of elevator pitches, write your own for each of the three. You can also take an extra step and "field test" your pitches with professional acquaintances and collect their feedback.

NOTES ON YOUR
ELEVATOR PITCH

Professional Pitch:

_____
_____
_____
_____

Future Pitch:

_____
_____
_____

Personal Pitch:

_____
_____
_____
_____

CHAPTER TWO

The Power of Your Strengths

*The best gift anyone can give, I believe,
is the gift of sharing themselves.*

–OPRAH WINFREY

Maya worked at a large company in a middle management position. She excelled at analyzing the corporate numbers in terms of how they impacted the bottom line. More importantly, she always came up with great ideas for proactive initiatives to minimize expenses and maximize profits. She enjoyed the work, and her supervisors respected her for that valuable ability.

But in the wake of criticisms that the organization lacked DEI programs, Maya's professional world suddenly rocked. The CEO realized they needed someone to jump-start that kind of effort in a newly created executive position. Because Maya was one of the few people of color (POC) members of the management team, she was chosen for the job. This was even though she had no experience in the DEI arena other than what she had experienced as a Black woman.

Suddenly, Maya was floundering in a job she never trained for, let alone asked for. She was a financial analyst, not a DEI expert. How was she supposed to know what to do? Her sense of herself as a competent person who got things done was shattered. She started to dread coming to work. At the same time, the company suffered from being deprived of the real contributions she made in her former position. But they didn't consider giving Maya her old job back. They assumed that would seem like a demeaning demotion. Ultimately, the new DEI role was eliminated for an outside consultancy service, and Maya had to look elsewhere for a job more suited to her qualifications.

Both the company and Maya were negatively impacted by the misguided attempt to emphasize her identity over her strengths in the workplace. The company lost the benefits from those strengths, and Maya struggled in a high-profile job in which she was not set up for success.

Understanding Strengths-Based Development

The above story illustrates how easily identity can trump the talents someone brings to the workplace. Maya may have originally regarded what happened to her as a positive. It involved a significant promotion, and who doesn't like that? Unfortunately, if you're "promoted" into a job where you are not set up to succeed, it's hard to create a positive outcome. It was never good when the people in charge were proclaiming, "I don't see color"—but acting from the standpoint of "All I see is color (or gender or sexual orientation or any combination of those identity factors)" can be just as harmful.

Maya's problem was she wasn't allowed to lean into her strengths, which severely undercut her effectiveness. The truth is your strengths are the foundation of your power, and they can be leveraged to give you power in the corporate world. When you show your strengths, that is, your natural talents and abilities, and the people in charge see how much you're capable of, it's much easier to make a name for yourself in that culture. After all, a company *needs* people with all kinds of talents, so your next step on this journey will be to determine how best to use what you've got to get what you want. It's time to uncover your superpower.

🔒 **UNSPOKEN RULE:**

Success comes from amplifying your strengths, not fixing your weaknesses.

What's good about that mission is it fits in with a lot of corporate thinking these days—it's more a spoken code than an unspoken one. It's easy to see why companies want to help employees develop their strengths. The research overwhelmingly shows it's a big positive for any company.[45] That's why, over the past six decades, a movement called Strengths-Based Development has taken hold in many work-places, centering on building up people's abilities rather than picking apart their weaknesses.

Strengths-based psychology, or focusing on what's right with people instead of what's wrong with them, was the brainchild of Don Clifton, a psychologist and professor at the University of Nebraska-Lincoln. He and a group of colleagues launched the Nebraska Human Resources Foundation in 1949, developing what was first called the "Clifton Strengths Finder," now the "Clifton Strengths Assessment." It has since been completed by over thirty-one million people and used by over 90 percent of Fortune 500 companies.[46] In 1999, Dr. Martin Seligman, then president of the American Psychological Association, furthered the concept by endorsing the approach when he stated, "The most important thing we learned was that psychology was half-baked. We've baked the part about mental illness, about repair damage. The other side's unbaked, the side of strength, the side of what we're good at."[47]

In the 1990s, the Strengths-Based Approach began to seep into business management and remains popular today. It seems like common sense for management to focus on helping people improve their strong points rather than attempting to "fix" their weaknesses, which is rarely effective. For example, imagine you had no musical ability, but someone insists on teaching you how to play the piano. How will that work out? Maybe you'll be able to bang out a passable version of "Chopsticks" but not much else. And yet, traditionally, managers have been quick to point out and focus on what their people are doing wrong instead of recognizing what they're doing right.

Strengths-Based Development flipped the script by acknowledging that we are all better at some things than others and that we would be happier and more productive if we spent more time focusing on what we're good at. Again, the research bears out the wisdom of this approach. Gallup, a global analytics and advisory firm, which was acquired by Dr. Don Clifton (and where, full disclosure, I worked for three years), studied thousands of work teams and millions of leaders, managers, and employees to understand how well this management approach works. They examined six outcomes: sales, profit, customer engagement, turnover, employee engagement, and safety. On average, workgroups that switched to a strengths-based intervention significantly improved on all these outcomes compared with control groups that received less intensive interventions or none at all. Ninety percent of the strengths-based workgroups enjoyed these positive results:

- 10 percent to 19 percent increase in sales

- 14 percent to 29 percent increase in profit

- 3 percent to 7 percent higher customer engagement

- 6 percent to 16 percent lower turnover (low-turnover organizations)

- 26 percent to 72 percent lower turnover (high-turnover organizations)

- 9 percent to 15 percent increase in employee engagement

- 22 percent to 59 percent fewer safety incidents

Finally, 67 percent of employees who truly believe their management focuses on strengths and positive characteristics feel strongly engaged with their job. In sharp contrast, only 2 percent of employees who don't share that belief feel engaged.[48]

Again, this just makes sense. When your job emphasizes tasks you don't like to do or aren't good at it, part of you rebels. It's unpleasant, and you feel like your real talents and abilities aren't being recognized or respected, especially if no one above you has ever had a conversation about them with you. But that's only half of the equation. The other side is that you may not know your own strengths. And that means you may be missing an opportunity to use those strengths to advance your career, because leaning into your abilities is the best way to show up in the workplace.

Identifying Your Strengths (and Weaknesses)

Many people are unaware of what they're naturally good at and what abilities they need to develop. I had this experience in grad school, where I discovered that the culture I was raised in had rewarded me mostly for fulfilling existing tasks and responsibilities. Growing up, I studied hard, did well in school, and felt like I was following the path expected of me. What I hadn't learned was how to color outside the lines. I rarely took initiative in seeking out new ways of doing things or taking actions that weren't already expected or assigned to me. Yet, graduate school required more of me than simply studying hard and regurgitating information. I was expected to understand the academic work that came before me, but the real task was to add value by creating my interpretations of the business world. Getting past my self-imposed rigidity was a personal breakthrough and necessary to have the career I wanted.

This is why I suggest you make it a mission to assess your strengths and weaknesses. This is a must if you hope to achieve any power and influence in the workplace. When you know and appreciate your strengths, you can create strategies to leverage them. For example, if writing is your strong suit, you can use your hand for assignments requiring that skill. If you communicate better through speaking instead of the written word, you can seek out opportunities to make a splash by delivering effective presentations and speeches. This kind of emphasis on your strengths empowers you to search for situations where you can make your mark and demonstrate the kind of superior performance that will make the higher-ups see you in a new and more favorable light.

🔒 **UNSPOKEN RULE:**

Seek opportunities to align your work with your strengths.

To do this, however, requires a strength-based mindset where you fully embrace what you're good at and either learn how to manage the things you're not so good at or work on the areas where you're capable of significant improvement, as I did. To return to Maya's story, she could have succeeded in that position if she had had the proper training leading up to her promotion. However, the higher-ups threw her into the deep end and expected her to be able to magically swim.

So, how do you assess your strengths if you're unsure what they are? You might want to make your first stop the CliftonStrengths® assessment I mentioned earlier. While this tool, offered by Gallup, is not free, it's a valuable resource, as it is based on their thirty-plus years of robust research.

However, you can also do this kind of assessment, starting by simply self-reflection. Begin by thinking about things you were naturally good at as a child. For example, a very talkative child who always gets in trouble for that trait can grow up to be a great public speaker for their team. Look at what came naturally to you, and determine how that talent can apply to your working life. You also want to look at the times when you felt like you were in flow when you were doing something, and you got so into it, you forgot to look at the time. When you finally did, you were amazed that hours went by without you realizing it. Being in flow indicates you're doing something you love to do and are good at. That's why you don't feel compelled to look for distractions or take breaks.

Another great way to assess your strengths is by having a frank discussion about them with other people. Ideally, that discussion will take place with people you trust, whom you also work with, and who have witnessed firsthand how you operate on the job. They can provide the right kind of focused feedback. The most important quality you have to look for in these talks, from both yourself and those you're engaging with, is honesty. People love to tell you what you're good at, but most will be far more reluctant to tell you the areas where you aren't so good. Be prepared (and unafraid) to press them a little.

Another person who should be aware of your strengths is your manager. If they are skilled at what they do, they should have a broad understanding of what you're good at simply by observing you doing your job over time and asking the right questions. Still, in most cases, they won't just volunteer that assessment unless they actively engage in Strengths-Based Development. That means, to get their (hopefully) valuable thoughts on your strengths, you'll probably need to ask for *directed* feedback from them,[49,50] because when they hear the word "feedback," most managers immediately leap to whatever it is you don't do well. However, it shouldn't be hard to ask what they think your strengths are, and there's no need to wait for your yearly review to make that request.

The bottom line is this: working from your strengths energizes you because it feels good to be doing what you excel at, and they also help you stand out. Remember that example of the would-be piano player with no musical ability I referenced earlier? If that person had enormous musical skills, they would quickly find they really enjoyed playing the piano because it's exciting to uncover that talent in yourself and see what you can do with it. The same result could happen when you've assessed your strengths in a meaningful way and begin to apply them in the workplace.

However, there is another big factor to consider when it comes to strengths, and that's identity.

Identity and Strengths

As I said, the research is sound when it comes to the power of Strengths-Based Development. However, that research is lacking in one substantial area, and that's applying it to anyone who isn't a white, cisgender, heterosexual male. That has obviously been the dominant group throughout history when it comes to American business, so that's the perspective baked in the cake of these types of studies.

White men have traditionally had more freedom to explore and leverage their best qualities, because they're already operating from a place of strength.[51] They're used to being in charge. I don't say this from a place of anger or judgment. I say it because it's been the default reality and still largely is despite some real progress in recent years. Even today, most of the people who make it to the C-suite are white men (57 percent, according to the latest McKinsey research[52]).

For the rest of us, we can have a difficult time understanding just what makes us individually awesome in the workplace, and the reason for that is easy to understand: we get the message from an early age that we have to work *twice* as hard to get *half* as far in so many areas of life. This means we give an inordinate amount of attention to the inevitable struggle we have when we discover that the modern corporate workplace was not made for us. By only using a strengths-based approach, you may assume that struggle can be resolved if you leverage your strengths properly. A critique of strengths development and positive psychology is that it assumes a causal relationship to well-being and goal achievement without regard to social status and identity.[53]

Perhaps strengths alone could level the playing field if we were all truly integrated into the workplace at every level. But that day has still not arrived. That's why some scholars posit the strengths-based development approach has a blind spot regarding ethnic, cultural, and other identity-related differences.[54] I experienced this tension between strengths and diversity firsthand while writing Gallup's first diversity and inclusion perspective paper in 2018.[55] It motivated me to have some very real conversations with the senior leadership team to explain that while the strengths assessment is a strong tool, it is strictly a tool, not a miraculous answer to the challenge of DEI. Ultimately, leadership agreed, and strengths became *part* of the company's approach to diversity and inclusion, not the whole story.

But you're probably asking, isn't a strengths assessment necessarily objective? Yes and no. We all may get the same assessment result, but how we view the world and how we came to acquire those strengths, or even how those strengths were viewed in our backgrounds, are very different.

For example, one of the strengths the assessment is designed to uncover is Command. People high in Command instinctively take charge and openly express their opinions. They genuinely feel they can calm the chaos. Only a tiny percentage of people in the world possess this trait to a great degree. For a man to be told he has this attribute, it's great news. Most *want* to feel like they are strong leaders. But when a woman is told she has Command, it's a little more complicated because, culturally, it's never been regarded as a desirable female trait. So, a woman who *does* possess high Command may seek to deliberately downplay it because she doesn't want to come off as "bossy" or another "b" word I won't repeat here.

Research verifies that women can be insecure about their strengths. Hewlett-Packard (HP) conducted an internal study in the early 2000s that found men are confident applying for a job where they meet only 60 percent of the qualifications. In contrast, women apply only if they meet 100 percent of them![56] So our backgrounds and identities impact how we perceive our strengths, as well as how others perceive them. It's not as cut and dried as simply knowing our strengths. Like anything else that attempts to be purely factual, there's an undeniable real-world component, and we need to find ways to account for that component.

Gaining Strengths through Struggles

At the same time, if we focus on strengths, we must consider the skills we gain from making our way in the corporate space despite our identities. Think about it. When faced with being othered, we must learn to talk to different people in different "languages." We also begin to understand the unwritten rules and the codes that are ever present in the working world that white males may not even be aware of because it's business as usual for them. That in itself is a kind of a gift and another strength we can lean into. I know I have.

With that in mind, know that your unique life experiences have cultivated some strengths in you that you didn't even realize were strengths. For example, if you're a person who has navigated a disability all your life, you see the world very differently from someone who hasn't had to. Maybe it means you've acquired more empathy and developed strong problem-solving skills simply because you've had to learn how to cope with different challenges than most. A positive perspective doesn't eradicate the difficulties you've experienced, but it is important. It's more productive for that person with a disability to avoid focusing on the negatives and instead look at how they can leverage what they've gained from their life experience. Their sharpened problem-solving ability may be an area they can invest in when pursuing a specific promotion or entering a new industry.

Army veteran and current program manager in tech, Brittany Wzontek, shared this experience with me:

The Army gave me a lot of skills as a generalist and being able to dive in and work really hard, but having to learn a whole new technical language very rapidly presented a huge challenge, and I often found myself feeling like an outsider because I wasn't from the tech industry, so I couldn't really speak the same language. I was the only woman on the team too.

So, I was surprised when after only four months I was asked to mentor someone who had been on the team for five years. They were very knowledgeable, but they were risk-averse and couldn't handle pressure and stress. I was asked to mentor them even though I personally felt like I had no idea what I was doing. I remember my boss saying, "You know how to handle stressful situations, and I know I can give you a task and you will run with it. I need you to mentor this person. Our team progress is stalling because they are too afraid to take risks." That was a moment I was grateful for my identity, that I was able to build that skill from my time in the military.

In this way, your identity can be your superpower, and your challenges in life can be growth opportunities. It's great you made it through whatever struggles you've managed to overcome, but the way to make those struggles meaningful to the rest of your life is to actualize the strengths you've developed and make them work for you professionally.

I also want to stress that deciding to focus on your strengths shouldn't mean you excuse all your weaknesses. For example, if you have trouble being on time, you can't just shrug it off and tell everyone, "Hey, I'm always late, so don't expect me to be punctual." The truth is you must show up on time for work! Whether your organization tells you punctuality matters or not, that's a rule everyone knows. Flagrantly disregarding it will catch up with you, and you'll be seen as undependable, disorganized, and possibly even disrespectful of other people's time.

Further, we know the corporate playing field is not created equally, and your identity can impact how certain behaviors are viewed. For example, one research study showed lateness behaviors are viewed differently for Black, white, and Hispanic employees, with the penalizing effect on advancement opportunities applying only to Black employees.[57] This is an unfair reality, but understanding these implications will help you navigate them better.

> 🔒 **UNSPOKEN RULE:**
>
> Own your flaws, and turn stumbling blocks into
> stepping stones for success.

With that in mind, the goal should be to be aware of and manage your weaknesses so that they don't prevent you from succeeding. For example, if you are a chronically late person, maybe you have to set alarms to keep yourself on schedule or find an accountability buddy who's going to call you on the way to work to make sure you're awake and aware. Having said that, you also shouldn't strain yourself to be the first to arrive for everything, because that's not how your energy should be spent. It should instead be invested in the strengths that will make you shine.

Owning Your Strengths

I'm Ella. I'm great at facilitating difficult discussions between people, and that's recently led me to getting an excellence in teaching award at Georgetown.

This statement is one I make when I want to put my strengths out there right away. I change it up depending on the situation, but the idea is to own your strengths by verbalizing them. To avoid bragging, keep your strengths statement factual and to the point, and explain how your strengths can add value to them or the team.

Also, understand that you should continue developing your strengths. At Gallup, many of us would make "strength resolutions" instead of New Year's resolutions. People would select a strength to work on for the year. For example, someone might decide to work on being more disciplined or enhancing their communication skills. This kind of effort helped them grow and improve.

The idea is that just because you're born with strengths doesn't mean you stop developing them. Instead, you keep investing in them to make them as robust as possible. That development may require some help, and you shouldn't be afraid to seek it out. Professional athletes have trainers, singers have vocal coaches, and actors have acting coaches. The idea that people make it entirely on their own is a myth that robs many deserving people of their chance to take their strengths as far as they can go.

🔒 UNSPOKEN RULE:

Success is a team sport. Every star had a wingman or backstage hero who made the win possible.

It's important to have a partner in your development, simply because you need an outside and experienced view. That partner should be someone who can help you see the whole picture in terms of where you currently are and where you need to get to with your skills. Having an accountability partner—someone who pushes you forward just as you push them forward—can be great because they don't cost you anything. Just find a peer at the same level as you whom you trust, and then find ways to support each other.

Another option is to find a mentor who has traveled the same paths as you and understands your challenges. This is someone at a higher level who can provide you with inspiration, advice, and a road map to get you where you want to be.

Finally, if you can afford it, I suggest you hire a professional coach, as they will be experienced in getting clients to the next level in their careers. Many people hesitate to pay for professional coaching, but someone with the right credentials and background can enormously benefit your professional journey. If professional coaching is cost-prohibitive to you, check to see if your organization might finance it for you—many companies invest in the professional development of their people.

Things to Remember

1. Assess your own strengths. You can accomplish this by seeking feedback from your peers, managers, friends, and family. You can also use online tools to identify your assets. Knowing your strengths is the next step in understanding your story. The more you understand yourself, the better you'll be able to navigate your career and interactions with others.

2. Leverage your strengths. Look for professional opportunities to take advantage of those strengths and help you shine in the workplace. Create quick fact-based statements that capsulize your talents.

3. Develop your strengths. Focus on improving them through personal efforts. Also, look for outside help by recruiting accountability buddies and mentors and hiring professional coaches.

CHAPTER EXERCISE: SUPERSIZE A STRENGTH

I related how, at Gallup, our New Year's resolutions would center on developing one of our strengths in the coming year. I recommend trying this approach but shortening the timeline and doing it over six months.

Six-Month Activity: Strengthening Success Journal

Reflect on Your Strengths (Month 1): Reflect on your strengths journal about specific instances where they contributed to your achievements. Seek feedback to gain deeper insights.

Strategic Opportunities (Months 2–3): Actively seek out and engage in professional opportunities that align with your strengths. Document your experiences, and create concise, fact-based statements, highlighting the impact of your strengths in these situations.

Personal Development Plan (Months 4–5): Create a personalized development plan outlining specific actions and milestones to enhance each identified strength. Recruit accountability buddies, and explore mentorship opportunities.

Reflect and Reassess (Month 6): Reflect on your progress. Assess how leveraging and developing your strengths has influenced your career and interactions. Create a "strength statement" that reflects what you learned.

One final aspect of this exercise: Create a "strengths statement" like mine, which I shared earlier in the chapter: *I'm Ella. I'm great at facilitating difficult discussions between people, and that's recently led me to get an excellence in teaching award at Georgetown.* In a couple of sentences, this statement should define your primary strength and validate it by mentioning an achievement you've reached through that strength.

In the next chapter, we'll explore what it means to be authentic in the workplace and how you can show up as a truer version of yourself.

YOUR STRENGTH STATEMENT

_____

_____

_____

_____

Recent success using this strength: _____

_____

_____

_____

Ways I want to invest in this strength: _____

_____

_____

_____

How I will hold myself accountable: _____

_____

_____

_____

What will progress look like (i.e., how will I know when I've gotten better)?

_____

_____

_____

NOTES ON STRENGTH

<u>What have been your experiences leveraging your strengths at work?</u>

CHAPTER THREE

Authenticity and Code-Switching

Against all odds I gave myself permission to take up space, knowing I belonged there no matter what anyone thought about me.

—SHERYL LEE RALPH

I was super nervous the first time I got braids while working in the corporate world.

Like many Black women, I get my hair braided in the summer months. I consider it a "protective style" to shield my hair against heat damage and everything else Black women put their hair through. But this time was different. This time, I was working at a big company where I was the only Black person in the office. So, when I was about to head into work with those braids for the first time, it almost gave me a nervous breakdown. I had so much anxiety about it that I texted my mentor, who happened to be a Black man, at six o'clock in the morning (which you should never do about a professional matter, but I was freaking).

I asked him how he thought I should play it. After all, they were going to notice that hair right away. I also had a client meeting that day. Would that be OK? Now, mind you, I didn't have a plan for what I would do if he said it *wasn't* OK. I couldn't take the braids out because it took six hours to finish them! I suppose if he told me this wasn't the best idea, I might have called in sick. But his response was, "You are professional. No matter what hairstyle you have, you'll be fine. Don't worry about it; I'm sure you look great."

I was so relieved. I got my confidence back and went into the office. The moment I sat down at my desk, one of the partners on my team, an older white male, walked by. He stopped at my desk. He looked at me. And he said, "Oh, your hair is interesting." And then he laughed and moved on. I was mortified. I felt so othered. The feeling was so intense I can still remember it, and this happened over a decade ago. All the positivity my mentor had gifted me with earlier evaporated instantly.

And here's the saddest part; that man probably meant it as a compliment at best or just a dumb joke at worst. I'm sure he forgot he said it almost immediately and had no idea that those five words hit me so hard. He probably never thought about it again—as opposed to me, who has thought about it hundreds of times the past decade.

Me bringing my identity into the workplace that day took its toll, as it does for so many others every day of their working lives.

The Challenge of Authenticity at Work

"Authenticity" is a big buzzword in the corporate world because of the many positives it brings to workers and companies that encourage it.[58]

Those positives are substantial for those who feel they can relax and be who they are in the workplace. After all, if you can't be your best self, you can't do your best work. Your best self is your *real* self. That's the version of you that brings your best ideas, questions, focus, energy, and passion. You and your job will suffer if you cannot be that person.

Almost everyone struggles with authenticity in the workplace, not just people with nondominant identities. A 2023 report from Deloitte found that even white men "cover" at work: "I try to avoid associations with the stereotypical, straight, cisgender, male archetype."[59]

🔒 UNSPOKEN RULE:

Everyone code-switches at work (to some degree).

In fact, research shows there is a relationship between authenticity, well-being, and work motivation;[60] it also says that authenticity at work and healthy psychological functioning are mutually reinforcing, leading to better performance on the job.[61] That's the good news. The bad news is that strain, distress, and maladjustment frequently stem from the dissonance caused by your identity bumping up against external experiences that make you feel you must behave differently to fit in. And when that dissonance is a large part of your life, it becomes exhausting and cognitively laborious, depleting personal resources.[62] In other words, feeling compelled to hide who you are can disrupt your whole career.

A 2021 *Harvard Business Review* article by Dr. Kathy Phillips and colleagues told the story of Marcus (a pseudonym), a Black man who joined a leading international bank right out of college. To him, the secret of success was simple—keep your head down, perform, and be rewarded. He did all those things, and clearly, he was successful, as evidenced by the awards he received for his results—and yet, he kept being overlooked for promotions.

But here's the thing. He wasn't being held back because he was Black. He was being held back because he was an enigma to his coworkers at the office. When he finally found the courage to ask his boss why he was being overlooked, the answer he got was almost shocking. "You're really good at your job, but the problem is that the partners feel they don't really know you." In that moment, he realized he had been hiding who he was at the office, afraid of being ostracized for his identity. He shifted gears and worked to overcome that fear, by making it a priority to seek out social opportunities with the partners and finding common areas of interest—kids, sports, and so forth. The result? Today, he is a managing partner.[63]

Marcus, like me, didn't know what was OK and not OK at the office. Each workplace has its own generally unspoken rules about how individuals believe they should act and present themselves at work, and those are typically informed exclusively by the dominant group's values and norms. Therefore, people like me, who usually don't belong to the dominant group, tend to adjust how we present ourselves. Our need to fit in narrows our behavioral options, which goes directly against corporate edicts to show up as "real."

Marcus didn't know when it was OK to be himself. He didn't know what might come back to haunt him. I felt the same way. I didn't know if it was OK just to show up at work with a new kind of hair. That's why, if you're in a nondominant identity, you can easily feel off-balance on the job, depending on the organization and the nature of your work. And you're not crazy for feeling that way!

As Kathy Phillips and colleagues put it, "Decades' worth of studies have shown that similarity attracts—a phenomenon known as homophily … being one's true self, disclosing elements of one's personal life, and forming social connections are easier within one's own group than they are across a demographic boundary such as racial background. This is crucial to keep in mind as companies aspire to become more diverse. Simply hiring members of a minority group won't ensure that they feel comfortable or equipped to build the relationships necessary for advancement."[64]

My experience, and that of many others, backs that up. When you show up as "different" in the eyes of the majority, others will point this out to you. And it could trigger you, just as a bland comment on my hair being "interesting" felt like a psychological body blow that haunts me to this day.

You might think it was silly to be that anxious about my braided hair. But believe me, I am far from alone. Take the case of award-winning comedy writer Amber Ruffin, who has written Broadway hits, hosted her own NBC show, and writes for the Seth Meyers talk show. You'd think someone breathing in that kind of rarified professional air would be past feeling anxiety over a new hairstyle. But she's not. As she writes in the hilarious and heartbreaking book, *The World Record Book of Racist Stories*,[65] "You have changed your hairstyle. It cost six hours and minimum $150. You go to work and as you get out of the car, the realization sets in—this will be the topic of conversation for the rest of the day. You make the dreaded walk from the parking lot to the door, knowing the dumbass questions are about to flow."

Like I said, you're not crazy.

Every group has their "danger zone," those aspects of their background that will inevitably draw unwelcome attention. A Sikh's turban. A Jew's yarmulke. Anyone's foreign accent. Someone transitioning. Even if a coworker or even a supervisor merely points these things out without much, if any, judgment attached, it makes the person on the other side of the remark feel othered. Unfortunately, it's just part of human nature. There is always a downside in being seen as somehow "different" from everyone else.

So how do you navigate your work life if you have these kinds of feelings? How much do you suppress, and will that suppression hurt you? Conversely, how much do you show, and will expressing yourself honestly hurt you?

Let's look at some strategies that can help you cope with what everyone agrees can be an extremely stressful and long-term problem for a professional.

Code-Switching

Growing up in North Carolina, I was drawn to the rap artist J. Cole, who also comes from there and speaks to my experience. I remember driving to my first corporate job as a first-year consultant, listening to J. Cole to get energized for my day. And every time I arrived at the building and pulled into the parking garage, I would automatically turn my music down or switch to something else. I didn't want my coworkers to see me listening to rap music. I didn't want them to think, "Oh, she's *that* kind of Black person."

The moment I turned the volume down, I was code-switching.

The term "code-switching" was initially coined in the 1950s by linguist Einar Haugen.[66] He used it to describe the ability to move between languages and dialects, but today, it has come to mean changing something (or multiple things) about yourself, like the way you talk, dress, or, yes, style your hair, to fit in with a more dominant group.[67] Even a white male who is eccentric in one way or another will attempt to hide an aspect of himself that he feels others will look down on. All of us code-switch to some degree. You probably behave differently at a job interview than you would with a group of your closest friends (or at least you should!).

However, the plain truth is people from nondominant groups do it far more frequently—because they feel the need to hide or downplay parts of their identities. A gay person would rarely admit their sexual orientation back in the day unless they were in an LGBTQ-friendly environment. As for people of color, we've been code-switching long before we had a term for it. For descendants of slavery, code-switching goes back to when enslaved people had to act subservient to their white masters or suffer horrific consequences. Even today, code-switching can be for safety. Ask any Black parent who has had to give their son "the talk" about how to behave if the police ever stop them. Code-switching is pretty much baked into the cake for people like me, especially in the workplace. But the same holds true mostly for anyone who isn't a member of the dominant group, which, in the workplace, still tends to be white, cisgender, heterosexual men.[68]

In my interview with Brian Baker, chief people officer at a global consulting firm, he shared:

> *Oftentimes, I see the unspoken rules as the things people have gotten away with for years, that the organization needs to move away from but are often invisible. And yet those rules are incredibly impactful in ways that usually are not good.*

Given authenticity is supposedly prized in the corporate space today, code-switching is often regarded as a negative term. But I think code-switching gets a bad rap. I see it as a tool that can be deployed strategically, like anything else. In fact, people who know how to code-switch effectively can better understand and meet the needs of various stakeholders like clients, business partners, and diverse team members.

The underlying challenge in code-switching is that if I feel like I *have* to turn my music down in the parking lot or turn into something that I think is more respectable or accepted, that isn't me. I'm not being who I am. However, if I am code-switching because I *want* to use it as a tool in the workplace environment, that's different. That's *strategy.* And strategy is what helps you circumvent unspoken rules and achieve better outcomes. Meaning, properly deployed, code-switching is a cheat code that empowers you to connect with different people in different ways.

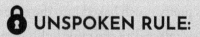

🔒 UNSPOKEN RULE:

Code-switching can be a strategy.

However, while code-switching is a tool when it's helping you get ahead, it's more like a muzzle when it's holding you back—or creating the kind of anxiety I felt when I would turn down the music on my car radio. That's when code-switching becomes oppressive, exhausting, and self-defeating. For that reason, it's important to discern between when you're showing up as anything other than your authentic self as a tactical move and when you're doing it because you think you wouldn't be welcome just being who you are.

An example of the first would be learning a sport like tennis, golf, or pickleball because you know the higher-ups at your company play it. Taking on a new game has nothing to do with repressing "the real you." After all, you're gaining a new skill and creating the conditions for bonding with people who could have your career in their hands.

That's strategic code-switching. An example of the second would be repressing your sexual identity. Certainly, it's your right not to talk about your dating life at the office, and nobody should force you into that kind of dialogue. However, if you're avoiding that kind of conversation because you're dating a same-sex partner and you don't think that will be accepted, that's fear-based code-switching. And that costs you in the long run.

The Downside of Code-Switching

While, yes, code-switching can be a useful tool, it's one you shouldn't lean on too hard. There's a big reason for limiting code-switching in the workplace and other aspects of your life. As I've already touched on in this chapter, too much code-switching wears you down, especially when you find yourself in a workplace that's not culturally diverse. I know this firsthand because that's the situation I was in when I had the panic attack about my hair braids and when I made it a point to turn down my car radio when I entered the office's parking lot. But it can be worse than that.

What if you feel you must change how you normally talk? For instance, you might attempt to "turn off" your accent because you don't want people to perceive you as too "foreign" or too ethnic or from the wrong region. I once had a coaching client in tears from the mental and physical exhaustion she said it took to turn off her accent at work day in and day out. That's an effort that uses up a great deal of thought and energy that could be better directed toward your actual job.

It's not hard to find people who feel the burden of code-switching. The *Harvard Business Review* article cited earlier contained the anonymous story of a Black man who also felt depleted by the same kind of situation I had to navigate:

One 32-year-old digital marketing assistant noted that his worst job was at an organization where the culture was not diverse: "The strain I endured as a person of color just trying to fit in was so taxing," he said, "that it negatively affected every other part of my life." But even though he's at an organization now that's more focused on diversity, he still struggles to find coworkers to bond with because of his previous experience.[69]

Code-switching can be especially stressful for individuals who already struggle with their mental health, as has been the case with Hailey Jade, a Korean American healthcare professional who suffers from depression and anxiety:

I am Korean American. I was raised in a very traditional Korean home, taught to always defer to my elders and not to speak unless I was asked a question. Through my life, those lessons have reinforced my natural shyness. I've been diagnosed with anxiety and panic disorder, but I always just thought I was extremely shy. Growing up in a Korean home, things like depression don't exist. As I became an adult, I realized that this was actually a condition.

During my MBA investment banking summer internship, I was forced to network and talk with senior leadership, and it was really uncomfortable. I knew I wasn't making any progress building my leadership skills. But since then, I've made a lot of progress. I made a goal to force myself to ask a question every single time there was a meeting with senior leaders. The first time I still remember shaking when I raised my hand. But we had these meetings twice a week, and by the time it was week seven I was ready to ask a question, and I realized it was becoming more comfortable. I also realized asking questions and asking for feedback helped me to perform better at work. I truly believe if you are honest about your weaknesses, people will believe you when you talk about your strengths.

As you can see, code-switching can weigh on you. And, by the way, if you think code-switching is a phenomenon that is diminishing with the continuing integration of cultures, research says otherwise. According to Pew Research, Black college graduates under fifty are likelier to feel it's necessary to code-switch. And four out of ten Black and Hispanic adults feel it's necessary to code-switch to succeed in their positions.[70] Of course, we need to be honest. Everyone has to code-switch to some extent. If you're a Democrat and your boss is a Republican or vice versa, you will probably temper your political opinions in front of them, even if you're white. However, people with nondominant identities feel the need to do it more often.

Then there is the snowballing effect of microaggressions, which are everyday insults or derogatory messages directed toward minorities and people of color, often from well-intentioned people who believe they've done nothing offensive. The "micro" part of the term misleads a lot of people to think these triggers are, in fact, small and meaningless. Well, they're not, and they can add up to "a host of mental health concerns, including things like increased anxiety and symptoms of depression."[71] In other words, it's like death by a thousand cuts.

If I spend two hours pondering if the partner who told me my hair was "interesting" was insulting me, I'm obviously not doing my best work for the next two hours. Not only that, but I also must consider if a remark like that in an almost all-white workplace is just the tip of the iceberg. Not a week goes by in the news cycle without someone somewhere uncovering racist emails traded by white supervisors who only talk that way between themselves and never openly to a Black employee. It's happened in government, law firms, police departments, and even universities. The people being ridiculed and "othered" by these authority figures can sense the undercurrent, even if they have no idea what's going on and it has a negative effect on them.

To show you just how someone who looks "different" can trigger those around them, let me tell you about a banking client ten years ago who hired me to do a diversity and inclusion talk. I soon discovered they were distraught because a white woman recently came to work with blue hair. They said it was unprofessional and distracting.

But was that true? Was the blue hair actually distracting to everyone? Or was the problem only that she looked different from the people sitting next to her? The employee eventually dyed her hair black to avoid further issues at work; sadly, she felt forced to downplay part of her identity for the comfort of others.

Tools for Managing Code-Switching

To sum up, authenticity is prized in the workplace these days. But, at the same time, code-switching is a useful and sometimes necessary tool. However, we also know that too much code-switching can negatively affect your job performance and even your health.

So, how do you know when to use code-switching and when you shouldn't?

In this last section, I want to talk about the delicate balancing act we all need to do, to find ways to show up authentically while not sabotaging ourselves by being real in a way that will harm us professionally. So, with that goal in mind, let me share some "cheat codes" that will be helpful to your approach.

UNDERSTAND WHY YOU'RE CODE-SWITCHING

When you code-switch, you want it to be a conscious decision, not just an unconscious fear or knee-jerk reaction. You must try to "read the room" (which we'll get into a little later in this book) as objectively as possible and then figure out what you need to do if you *want to* fit in as smoothly as possible.

For example, I generally appear younger than I am. I'm not complaining, but, since I teach, I do what I can to be viewed as more mature in that position, especially since I'm a Black woman. That makes me a minority in three different categories when I compare myself to other professors in business schools. I also know that women and people of color are more harshly evaluated on their teaching evaluations.[72]

That's why I got some valuable advice from another Black professor when I first started teaching. He told me, "You'll see a lot of your colleagues dress down. I would encourage you to dress up, otherwise your students will lean into, I wouldn't call it disrespect, but being more casual with you than you're probably comfortable with."

Now, no one told me to dress any type of way besides him. And I saw some of my white male colleagues choosing to wear jeans in the classroom. So, yes, I could have dressed any way I wanted to. But because I understood my situation (thanks to that professor), I chose to dress up for the classroom as a strategic code-switch. I will admit I do feel more confident when I'm dressed professionally, but I also wanted to heed the advice I had gotten and not let a casual dress make my students take me less seriously in my role.

That choice was a decision that wasn't necessarily right or wrong. It was a *self-aware* decision made from an objective thought process. I wanted to optimize my effectiveness in the teaching role, that's all, and what I wore wasn't a big deal to me. I judged the environment and made what I felt was an appropriate choice.

Recently, I spoke with private equity executive Donnie Bedney about the challenges he has faced showing up authentically as a Black man. He shared the following story:

A lot of people show up in a way that they believe that other people want them to show up. I think that happens a lot to people like us. I know I've been that way. I've always been taught to dress for the role you want. I remember having a conversation with my managing partner about growing out my facial hair. His statement was, "It's kind of an old wives' tale, but they always say, if you're working in sales, business development, or consulting, you can never trust a man if you can't see his face." I typically got a haircut every week and kept my face clean-shaven.

Then I had a fellowship where I spent four months in Nairobi, Kenya, serving as the chief operating officer for an HR technology startup. It was the first time in my life that I lived in a country where I was in the majority. My colleagues, who all were Kenyan, got a haircut, and that was the cleanest-cut they were until the next haircut weeks later. I made a decision that I actually was just going to show up how I wanted to show up, so I started growing my beard.

Looking back, I would argue that my experience there felt the equivalent of Superman's origin story. Living and working in Kenya allowed me to discover a side of myself where I could literally wake up and show up exactly how I wanted to, whether that was with a beard, or longer hair, or more relaxed clothing. And I never went back. I haven't worn a tie within a business setting in close to ten years now.

Of course, feeling different isn't limited to the way you look. Imagine you're in the break room with a bunch of coworkers and they all start talking about watching an episode of the *Ghosts* sitcom. If that happened to me, I would be lost because I don't watch that show. Now, I can choose to pretend I watch *Ghosts* and laugh along as if I had when someone starts rehashing jokes from the show. But that's not my best self, and there's no reason for me to do that code-switch. My favorite sitcom is *Insecure*, because I love Issa Rae. She's someone I really look up to. So, I would hope I would feel comfortable sharing that fact instead of acting like I watch the same thing as everyone else. If I never talk about me and my preferences, they'll never know, right? They get to learn my perspective, and I get to learn theirs. That's a growth opportunity for all of us.

What I'm saying here is pretty simple. Just be smart about your code-switching. Don't regard it as a suit of armor you always have to wear. Instead, see it as a shield to employ only in certain situations. Yes, be flexible and adaptable. After all, almost everyone in a workplace has to possess those qualities in order to work together successfully. Just don't betray your real self, and don't drown your authenticity in a sea of misguided accommodation. Do it in a way you're comfortable. That might be more than I do or less. But it's your life, and you should do what works best for you and your professional situation.

REMEMBER, FEELINGS ARE NOT FACTS

When I was scared to let people hear what was playing on my car radio, I was making a big assumption that others would judge me on my music. Was that a fact? No, that was a feeling. Same with my braids.

Everyone is sensitive about being judged. That goes double, triple, quadruple for those who have a nondominant identity, because they are conditioned to expect to be insulted or discriminated against.[73]

There is a trauma they carry around with them that gets easily triggered because of their lived experiences.

The result is you may feel like you're facing discrimination when it's not a cut-and-dried situation. Your feelings are valid because you've been burned in the past. But, again, you're making an assumption, which may or may not be wrong. And it's not good for your mental health to always assume the worst.

With one healthcare client I consulted for, there was a problematic employee who was Black. His supervisor shared that he was not performing at the level he should be in a role that literally could have meant life and death to someone. The employee pushed back and said he was being called out just because of his race. The supervisor replied that the data showed his lack of performance and had nothing to do with bias.

So, what's the reality?

This is someone who admitted he didn't feel seen during his performance review, or maybe the correct way to term it was he felt he was *only* seen as Black. But that may not have been true in this instance. It may be he needed the clear feedback as a wake-up call to help him improve. And if that was the case, he needed to know what that negative data was and act on it. However, it can *also* be true that the supervisor's approach lacked empathy.

This was hard to sort out, but I encouraged the supervisor, who was genuinely upset about the situation, to circle back to the employee in a few days and say something to the effect of, "Hey, I know we had a tense conversation last week about your performance and how it needs to be improved, but I also did hear you when you described your overall experience feeling ostracized throughout your whole career because you're Black. I'd like to hear more about your experience at this company and learn from it."

Two things can be true at the same time. This employee's performance may have been below par, *and* he could have felt uncomfortable as a Black man in a predominantly white workspace. The latter may have fed into the former. Ideally, the supervisor would examine the dynamics of their workplace, and the employee would reevaluate his track record and be honest about seeking out improvement.

The important thing is finding the courage to talk about these issues, saying the things you typically keep to yourself, and asking questions you might hold back. Unless you challenge your assumptions, you can't sort out what's true, and you will keep reacting unconsciously to situations you could be proactive about solving. So, when these feelings bubble up, try to be present, more comfortable with yourself, and more vocal in expressing your feelings.

REACH OUT AND BUILD RELATIONSHIPS

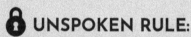

🔒 **UNSPOKEN RULE:**

Strong workplace relationships pave the way to
success.

Remember the story of the Black man who was repeatedly passed over for promotions, yet he didn't understand why? It was later discovered that the partners who managed the business had no knowledge of who he truly was, as he never felt comfortable sharing any details about his life with them. When this man realized this was how he was viewed, he made the effort to create social bonds with those partners and ended up becoming one himself.

Too often, we hold ourselves back from making new connections simply because we feel we won't be accepted as we are. But, again, that's a huge assumption. You might as well take the chance to start socializing with others because it might not be at all true. In any case, you'll discover whether or not you're working for a place that won't accept you, and knowledge, even of a negative thing, is power.

So be strategic as well as more human. Deepen your relationships with others. Maybe stop thinking about someone as just a professional colleague with whom you don't feel comfortable discussing your personal life, and try going to lunch with or just having some one-on-one conversations when the opportunity arrives. Some of my closest work colleagues have been incredibly different from me demographically and in terms of life experience-wise, but these are people I forged connections with, just by having a meal or grabbing a coffee.

Have an intention to build relationships on the job. You don't have to be best friends. You don't even have to talk outside of work if that isn't in the cards. You can still create a connection that will help you bridge your differences.

At the end of the day, we're all just people trying to do our best. But if you are feeling bad vibes on the job, don't assume that's the end of the road for you there. Yes, it might be a problem that's pervasive throughout this particular workplace—in that case, again, you might want to look for the exit door. But it just might be a case where you need to work on bonding with those around you.

Things to Remember

1. While authenticity is increasingly desired in the workplace, balancing authenticity with when you choose to code-switch can be a viable strategy.

2. Code-switching, when carried to an extreme, can be harmful to your job performance and even to your mental and physical health. By being judicious with code-switching and only using it strategically, you can reap its benefits without sinking under its drawbacks.

3. Try to limit code-switching to instances where you do it as a conscious choice, not a fear-based reaction. Don't assume the worst, and seek instead to clarify the situation when you feel you're being slighted. Finally, look for ways to feel more connected to the people you work with by sharing more about yourself and looking for positive social situations.

CHAPTER EXERCISE: WHERE ARE YOU CODE-SWITCHING?

Do you feel you're doing too much code-switching? How much of it is actually necessary? Is your code-switching forced or strategic? The following exercise will help you reflect on your code-switching behaviors, adapted from McCluney et al.'s Code Switching at Work Scale.[74]

Instructions: To what extent do you agree with the following statements about your behavior in the workplace? Response Scale: 1 = Strongly Disagree to 5 = Strongly Agree

1. I try not to dress in ways that draw attention to my identity. _____

2. I try not to act like other people who share my identity. _____

3. I try to make sure my hairstyle blends in with others at work. _____

4. I withhold opinions at work that draw attention to my identity. _____

5. I avoid behaviors that will make people at work think that I am different. _____

6. I avoid eating or bringing food to work that draws attention to my identity. _____

7. I go by a different name at work that does not draw attention to my identity. _____

8. I avoid sharing details about my weekend or free time that draw attention to my identity. _____

9. I intentionally show interest in activities that people of my identity group are not commonly associated with.

    _____

10. I consciously modify my communication style at work to match those of a different identity than me._____

Now, look at your answers to see where you have a lot of 4's and 5's and ask yourself if you are doing them:

- because you feel forced to,

- because it's your strategy, or,

- because it makes you feel comfortable.

Reflect on how you feel about the reasons behind your code-switching to determine if and how you might want to try showing more of your authentic self.

NOTES ON AUTHENTICITY AND CODE-SWITCHING

Reasons why I'm code-switching:

_____

_____

_____

_____

_____

_____

How I can show more of my authentic self:

_____

_____

_____

_____

_____

_____

SECTION TWO

How are you showing up in the workplace right now?

Examine the ways you experience and navigate your current space with others.

SECTION TWO

CHAPTER FOUR

Be Ready, Be Right, Be Excellent

If you want to play at an excellent level, if you want to do something excellent, you have to be excellent all the time. It's a way of life. It's not just you show up on Monday and be excellent. It doesn't work that way. You have to be excellent across the board. When excellence becomes a habit, that's just who you are.

–KOBE BRYANT

Kobe's words bring me back to the well-known "Black proverb" I've cited a few times in this book: "You've got to work twice as hard to get half as far." Granted, given his talent, twice as far for Kobe Bryant was further than most people who ever played the game. However, these words describe the experience many people with nondominant identities have when trying to compete in the workplace.

The origin of the aphorism is unknown, but for many years, it has strongly resonated with those who have felt, for legitimate reasons, that the deck was stacked against them. Unfortunately, economic data demonstrating Black men and women must have higher productivity than their white counterparts to be seen as equally skilled only further legitimizes these feelings of having to work twice as hard.[75]

In recent years, there has been some blowback against this thought, as articulated in this excerpt from a blog post by Lee Edward Colston II, an actor, writer, coach, and public speaker who holds an MFA from the Juilliard School:

We may sometimes find success by being "twice as good" but keeping that mask on, operating at that level all the time leaves little room for your humanity. It's exhausting. Your inevitable human mistakes and short comings will ultimately lead you to shame yourself for not being perfect in the eyes of white people and other Black folks who are watching; or at least that's what my experience was.[76]

He's not wrong. It *is* an exhausting way to think and just as exhausting as the perpetual code-switching we explored in the previous chapter. Again, we often bump up against unspoken rules that can be almost impossible to take on directly. So, what's our best cheat code against this stacked deck?

In this chapter, we're going to explore the art of excellence and how to leverage your talents and expertise in the workplace. I'll also share some special people's personal stories that reflect their experiences as well as their own proactive solutions to difficult workplace situations.

Committing to Your Best

One of those special people is Nzinga Shaw, an HR-DEI strategist, educator, and executive coach who has won numerous 40 Under

40 Awards and has held high-profile positions with such prestigious organizations as the Atlanta Hawks, Starbucks, and CAA, one of Hollywood's premiere talent agencies. She has spent years navigating the corporate space and shared these observations with me:

Extra relaxed behavior is not going to get you far in the workplace. That's an unspoken rule. There are also unspoken rules about nepotism. Sometimes Black and brown people get upset when we see white kids get an internship and they didn't even apply properly. Or someone's uncle is leading the account, so now they're on the team ... Is it fair? No. Is it dead wrong? Yes. But talking about it out loud, probably not smart. So, you should make the mental note that this is not a fair playing ground that we're on. And if they get someone in the door unfairly, you're gonna have to figure out ways to outshine that person. Let me make sure I'm leveling up my work. Let me make sure my work is better and smarter, so that I'm able to have proof points when it comes time for a performance review.

Committing to and upholding a standard of excellence in the workplace is crucial when navigating the unspoken rules. Assume if there's an excuse to hold you back from advancement, the powers that be will use it and do your best not to give them one. Personal excellence is another powerful cheat code that we can access daily.[77] Of course, it's not exactly cheating to do your best, but it is a definite path to progress in terms of making your mark in the workplace, no matter what your identity is. That doesn't mean we must burn ourselves out in the fruitless pursuit of perfection. Nobody can be perfect. Unfortunately, people sometimes confuse excellence with perfection, when it is more about doing the job as well as we can whenever we can. To be honest, that's what we should expect from ourselves, even without the complexities of identity.

> 🔒 **UNSPOKEN RULE:**
>
> **Excellence does not mean perfection. It means doing your personal best.**

I already shared how my mother "coached" me as a young girl. She always asked me the humbling question, "Did you do your best?" She didn't ask if I got an A or how everyone else did on a paper or a test. It was all about what I was capable of and if I was fulfilling my potential.

That question has stayed with me throughout my entire professional life and motivates me to live by this core tenet: be ready, be right, and *be excellent*. What does that mean? To me, it means you should be ready in the sense that you've planned, you're prepared, and you're armed with the knowledge you need to succeed. Be right in the sense that you've attained a high level of competency, you're professional, and you're rigorous about checking your work. And then, finally, be excellent in terms of being confident, consistent, unfailing, empowered, and committed to honoring what you know is your best. In other words, create your own standard of excellence, and stay true to that standard throughout your career.

You will still face unfair situations, and you may be overlooked or even dismissed by some. Niya Baxter, senior manager at a Big 4 consulting firm, who leads about ninety thousand professionals, remembers this early-career experience:

I was working with a senior manager, a white woman. I was a senior consultant at the time, and my manager would constantly present to the client in my place. She kept telling me I wasn't ready, so I would prepare the work, I would prepare her, and she would go do it, because I "wasn't ready." But then a white woman who was a peer to me joined my team. We were at a client retreat—one of the retreats where I had been told many times I was not ready to present. And pretty early on, this white woman was given the opportunity to present to these clients ... and it was a mess. She was underprepared. Her papers were all over the place. Her message was not good. I sat there and I watched her, and I watched the senior manager step in for her and save her during the presentation. I watched the grace that she was given on the back end to get a little bit of feedback and go and try again. Whereas for me, having been on the team for much longer than her, it was, "No, you're not ready." That was one of the earliest memories that I have in the professional space of understanding that for me to have the same opportunities, I had to be perfect and exceptional. I was not going to be given grace.

So yes, you will face setbacks. However, when you maintain an overall standard of excellence, you have a good chance of getting somewhere, just like Niya did. When you don't, you probably won't.

Identity

The late legendary actor Chadwick Boseman powerfully said, "When I stand before God at the end of my life, I would hope that I would not have a single bit of talent left, and could say, 'I used everything you gave me.'" These words delivered at Howard University's 2018 commencement are my guiding light.

It's apparent from his short but brilliant life that Boseman did just that. He gave it all he had, was true to himself, and, in the process, turned what might have been just another movie superhero into an avatar for hope and inspiration for all POC—even the entire world. I'm, of course, talking about the Black Panther movie, the twelfth highest-grossing movie of all time worldwide.[78] That Boseman could succeed on such a massive scale with this goal while battling colon cancer is a testament to his using every single bit of his talent because he didn't have an easy start by any means.

In that same commencement speech, Boseman talked about his early career, when he was cast in a popular network soap opera. The producers told him they wanted him around for a long time. He was promised he would make six figures, the first time that much money had been dangled before him—so he didn't feel he could say no. And yet, he soon found he was uncomfortable with the character he was supposed to play. As he relates,

I found myself conflicted. The role wasn't necessarily stereotypical ... but (it) seemed to be wrapped up in assumptions about us as black folk ... after filming the first two episodes, execs of the show called me into their offices and told me how happy they were with my performance. They said if there was anything that I needed, just let them know. That was my opening. I decided to ask them some simple questions about the background of my character, questions that I felt were pertinent to the plot. Question number one: Where is my father? The exec answered, "Well, he left when you were younger." Of course. OK. Question number two: In this script, it alluded to my mother not being equipped to operate as a good parent, so why exactly did my little brother and I have to go into foster care? Matter-of-factly, he said, "Well, of course she is on heroin."

Boseman was upset. The character seemed to be totally negative, and he suggested that the writers had made him "stereotypical." He asked that the character be given a positive trait that he could also work with. The meeting was done, handshakes were exchanged, and the next day, after he had taped a third episode, the bomb dropped. He got a call from his agent telling him he was being replaced.

The fact is, if you do have a nondominant identity, you will run into many obstacles in your career that white males won't, just as Boseman did.[79] Nzinga Shaw, whom I quoted earlier, related to me her story about how she starkly experienced the difference between an organization that was diverse and inclusive and one that definitely wasn't.

My very first job out of college was at Essence *magazine, which is a publication for African American women. After that, I went to the New York Yankees, which was a white male–dominated organization. At* Essence, *there was a lot more grace given when I made mistakes or needed help navigating corporate politics. I had a boss who was also African American who took me by the hand and said, "Hey, this is how things work." He shepherded me every step of the way. Whereas at the Yankees, there was no grace given when I made mistakes. People would communicate it to me in real time not in a way that was meant to give me constructive feedback—rather, it seemed meant to break my spirit and tear me down. I looked around to see how my white counterparts were given feedback, and it was very different. When I left the Yankees and went to the National Football League, I saw things exacerbated in terms of the way people of color were treated. We were not given priority positions, and we were often left out of the decision-making rooms, even though our titles indicated we should be there. I saw very quickly that there is not an even playing ground and there are different rules for different people.*

To be clear, things have improved in recent years, but studies show that improvement hasn't been fast enough or strong enough. Let me share some recent statistics:

- 77 percent of the US workforce is white.
- Only nine Fortune 500 companies have a Black CEO.[80]

- One in four Black and Latin employees report discrimination at work.

- Candidates with "distinctively Black names" have a lower probability of hearing back from companies they applied to in comparison to candidates with "distinctively white names."

- Despite making up half the workforce, women's wages equal only 83 percent of men's wages.

- Even when women have the same qualifications as men for a position, they are 30 percent less likely to be called for a job interview.

- Only one in six Fortune 500 companies publish annual DEI reports.[81]

The fact is if you have a different identity than the majority, you are usually held to a different standard—a much higher one. Because if you do make a mistake, or even if you don't, but something still goes off the rails, you will be judged more harshly. A recent, painful example of this phenomenon is the story of Dr. Claudine Gay, the first Black president of Harvard University, who was forced to resign over some minor attribution errors in her dissertation.

Dr. Gay's situation was unique and highly political in nature and too complex to detail here. I doubt many people reading this will someday find themselves the target of a US congressperson hoping to make a name for themselves. However, the fact that Dr. Gay was held to and lost her job because of an impossible standard of perfection no one is asked to meet in the real world serves as tangible proof that, yes, these biases do exist. Sometimes, we have to acknowledge that the system was not only not built for us but also works against us. In cases like this, the solution is not to be perfect because perfection is impossible. If someone is looking for imperfection because they're biased, they will find it, and no amount of readiness, rightness, or excellence will stop them. However, Lawyer Sydney Jacobs, a woman of color, found having the receipts to be helpful in one problematic workplace, as I learned when I interviewed her:

> *I once had a client project where my supervisor was pretty checked out. I was responsible for the day-to-day management. One time the client came to us with a project and only gave us a few days to get it done. I jumped on it immediately and gave it to the partner to review and approve, as I was supposed to, but she was not aware of the deadline, even though she had been copied on all the emails between me and the client. When I did submit it, she felt I had almost missed the deadline because she did not take the time to understand the client request before jumping to conclusions. Instead of coming to me about it, she went to other partners within our practice to complain about me and started this whole big thing ... which resulted in me having to explain myself to those partners and HR. I was livid, because the only reason why she was able to be that disengaged from this client was because I was doing my job and I was doing it well. I would not accept this misconception that I was about to miss this deadline. What I did was put together a timeline of every step I took to demonstrate that I was on top of it. I attached all emails to that timeline, which demonstrated she was copied on everything. Although this woman self-identified as my mentor, I had to stand up for myself because that just couldn't fly.*

Sydney Jacobs was ready, and she was right when the time came to prove her excellence. She hadn't dropped the ball, the partner had. And she calmly proved her case with the documentation that proved her truth.

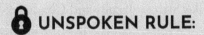

UNSPOKEN RULE:

Make sure you always have the receipts.

You must have your ducks in a row when you have a nondominant identity, and you should always have receipts. But this does not mean you should allow yourself to be demeaned or falsely attacked. You don't have to submit to false narratives, like Sydney Jacobs, nor do you have to submit to worn-out stereotypes, as Chadwick Boseman showed us. Yes, he lost his job just because he asked some questions, but if he was punished for that, imagine how debilitating the whole experience would have been if he had just stayed for the paycheck. Instead, he found greater fulfillment in his arena after that unfortunate experience because his excellence in his art was beyond reproach.

Overcoming Obstacles to Showing Your Excellence

When working in a workplace that's not receptive to your identity, it's easy to soak up the negativity and judgment accompanying that kind of attitude. Eventually, it can diminish your self-respect and make you feel like you're not good enough for whatever role you occupy.

However, if you're confident in yourself and your work, no one else should have the power to do that to you. Period. Yes, it will happen, but you don't have to accept an unfair assessment of you and your work. If you do buy into that negativity, you'll become a victim, and it will only get worse from there. The ideal tactic is to carry with you a sense of personal integrity in what you stand for morally and a high standard for your work and how you show up at the office. That's how you prevail like Sydney Jacobs and Chadwick Boseman did.

It can't be about other people. It must be about you and your self-regard. If you operate primarily out of frustration and anger about how someone treats you, you lose your standard of excellence. Instead, you want to run your own race to the very best of your ability while, at the same time, knowing that no one is always operating at 100 percent. Sometimes, all you have is 80 percent in the tank, thanks to all kinds of external factors—anything from a bad cold to a bad breakup. But that's OK. You're human, and you don't have to be perfect. But you do have to deliver at whatever level you're capable of on that day because the secret of this chapter's cheat code is that by showing up and delivering your best, you can more easily navigate shifting expectations.

🔒 **UNSPOKEN RULE:**

Delivering your best helps you navigate shifting expectations.

It can be difficult, but you can transcend a negative work experience if you don't give up on yourself. Instead, focus on creating your own opportunities for success in ways that suit your talents and temperament. And, by the way, this cheat code applies to *everyone* because I don't mean to imply white people are never at a disadvantage on the job. But you can overcome your disadvantage by looking for ways to stand out. For example, if you see a need where you work, or even just within your team, look for an innovative way to meet that need that leans into your strengths. Do that enough times, and you become unstoppable. But it does take work, intention, and effort—we'll talk about this more in depth a little later. For now, understand that the foundation is establishing a personal standard of excellence that you and those around you can count on.

Despite the politics and power dynamics, most workplaces like to believe they operate as meritocracies, and good work tends to get rewarded in some fashion. If you're strategic about your work and delivering at a high level, it will benefit you if you're recognized for it, which is the next key to this cheat code. The cliché "Work smarter, not harder" isn't wrong, but I would add a corollary: "Work in a way where you will get recognized for it."

🔒 UNSPOKEN RULE:

Work in a way where you will get recognized for it.

No matter how hard you work, if you keep your head in the sand, corporate America may not notice. You don't have to do jumping jacks in the break room to get people's attention, but you don't want to be shy about taking credit for something you've accomplished.

In the next chapter, we'll get to the necessity of what I call "reading the room." But let me touch on this idea a little bit here. To succeed in an organization, you must understand its dynamics deeply and see who rises to the top, who doesn't, and why. If you have an opportunity to learn from them one-on-one, seize it because you want to understand what excellence looks like in the environment that you're working in.

Every organization is different; every culture is different. Your job is to try to quantify what defines success within your company as much as you can. That's easy to do in a department like sales, where the numbers mean everything, but it's not so easy to pin down discernible metrics in many other roles. So, ask your manager to provide some metrics for what constitutes success in your position—some clearly defined targets you can focus on and hopefully meet. Have them write those metrics so that there is a paper trail. Along the same lines, always be prepared to show them the receipts. Create your own paper trail, just like Sydney Jacobs did when her boss claimed she dropped the ball. You want to easily dispel any suspicion that you did not do your best.

In the end, it may turn out you're not in the right environment or career to succeed. You must be honest in admitting that to yourself if that's the case, and you have to be motivated enough to find what *is* right for you. Look for the right opportunity for your personal fulfillment. Where's your passion? How do you line up your talents with that passion? These are crucial questions to answer.

Words to Live By

Be ready, be right, and be excellent. Those are words I live by to this day. Uncovering and understanding how to best position yourself for success in an organization will propel you forward, so take the time to figure out yourself and the environment you're working in. That time will no doubt pay off for you.

Near the start of this chapter, I shared some disturbing recent statistics regarding how those with nondominant identities are mistreated in the workplace. I want to close on some more positive numbers that demonstrate the power of a company that *does* embrace DEI initiatives. You'll see for yourself that when everyone is allowed to succeed at a company, everyone benefits, including the company itself.

- Diverse companies have 2.5 times higher cash flow per employee.

- Diverse management outperforms less diverse management.

- Companies with more than 30 percent women executives outperformed the others by 10 percent to 30 percent, while companies in the top quartile of racial and ethnic diversity outperformed by 36 percent compared to fourth-quartile companies.

- Companies with above-average total diversity had 19 percent higher innovation revenues and 9 percent higher EBIT (earnings before interest and taxes) margins on average.

- Diverse teams make better decisions 66 percent of the time. Gender-diverse teams were found to make better business decisions 73 percent of the time, while teams including a range of ages and different geographic locations saw better decisions 87 percent of the time.

- Employees who feel included within their organizations are about three times more likely than their peers to feel engaged and excited by organizational missions.[82]

Things to Remember

1. Over the long run, creating a personal standard of excellence and committing to it help pave your way. Seal the deal by making an impact so that it earns you recognition.

2. Discover the company's metrics for success you need to meet in your role and surpass their expectations if you can. Stay prepared and retain evidence of your efforts in case they're ever questioned. In short, be ready, be right, and be excellent.

3. Meet shifting expectations by remaining consistent. If you always deliver, you raise your value within an organization. If you're unhappy in your current role, tap into your passion and look for ways to fulfill it over time.

CHAPTER EXERCISE: DEFINE AND LEVERAGE YOUR STANDARD OF EXCELLENCE

Go back and revisit your own professional and personal successes. What was your process in those instances? Can you replicate that process in the future and create your standard of excellence by examining it? What do you need to do to compensate for your weaknesses? Or to make the most of your talents and knowledge? If you want, model yourself on a famous and successful person you admire, such as Oprah Winfrey, Steve Jobs, or even someone like Taylor Swift or Beyoncé. How did they get to where they were? What can you do to emulate their process and improve your own?

Also, look at what creates the conditions for you to be at your best at work. Do you require a certain amount of sleep? Should you back off on drinking or using other substances? Are there some steps you might want to take every morning before you go to work to empower you? Does working out or meditating energize you and help you focus?

Finally, get real with your manager, in terms of what they believe good performance looks like. Collect some concrete examples, get them to be as specific as possible, and have this conversation not just when you start in a new role. Have it multiple times such as after your first six months and after your first year, so you always know what excellence looks like in your environment. To get you started, here are ten questions to ask during your meeting:

1. What are your expectations for my role? Does my work meet your expectations? _____

    _____

    _____

    _____

2. What do you consider my strengths? _____

    _____

    _____

3. What do you consider my weaknesses? _____

    _____

    _____

4. What areas of improvement should I prioritize, and do you have any specific suggestions as to how? _____

    _____

    _____

    _____

5. How do you measure my performance? _____

    _____

    _____

6. How can I support my team better? _____

    _____

    _____

7. Do you feel I am focusing on the right things in my role?

    _____

    _____

    _____

8. What challenges is the company currently facing that I can help solve, and how? _____

_____

_____

9. What upcoming challenges is the company facing, and how might I help with those? _____

_____

_____

_____

10. What would you like to see from me before our next conversation? _____

_____

_____

In our next chapter, we'll look at how to "read the room" to understand the unspoken rules that are at play in your workplace.

NOTES ON STANDARD
OF EXCELLENCE

Define your personal standard of excellence:

_____

_____

_____

_____

_____

Have you noticed any Unspoken Rules
related to standards of excellence at your
current or past jobs?

_____

_____

_____

_____

_____

_____

CHAPTER FIVE

Read the Room

Let us not look back in anger, nor forward in fear, but around in awareness.

—JAMES THURBER

Let's say you know how to do what we talked about in the previous chapter, and be ready, be right, and be excellent. As a result, you bring everything you're capable of to your working environment.

However, that's only half the battle. Yes, you're prepared to give your best. But now you need another skill set to ensure your best is recognized and rewarded. That requires that you gain the ability to "read the room" to the point where you understand the dynamics of the organization you're working for, get insight into those you interact with, and have an awareness of the hidden signals that seemingly superficial communications are masking.

So, in this chapter, we're going to explore, through firsthand stories and revealing research, just how to read the room and know your audience. It's more important than you might think. After all, some of our most iconic geniuses and business legends have suffered as a result of a failure to develop that ability—including such luminaries as Steve Jobs (canned by Apple, the company he founded, which he eventually had to come back to rescue), Walt Disney (told he wasn't "creative enough"), Mark Cuban (disobeyed his boss), and Oprah Winfrey (told she wasn't "fit for television news"). Even the beloved TV chef Julia Child lost a job because of "gross insubordination."[83]

Yes, they all survived those indignities, but they had extraordinarily singular visions, skills, and drive to compensate for those setbacks. Most of us lack that "unicorn" energy, and as a result, it's important to learn how to read the people around us to prosper or, sometimes, just to plain survive. This chapter will provide the cheat codes to help you do that.

What They Don't Say

Kimberly Hogg Massey is a seasoned marketing veteran, having occupied executive roles in such global companies as PepsiCo and Kimberly-Clark. I interviewed her on this topic, and she provided some valuable insights into reading the room:

You've got to watch and be perceptive before you try to really work the room. I think some people mistakenly think, "I've got to be out there, talking and doing this and that," but there's immense power in listening intently and watching how people respond to other people and watching what they're saying versus what they're not saying with their body language. I got that advice early, and it has served me well. Picking up on people's cues is really important in corporate. It's a skill in itself. Anyone can learn the skill. You have to be aware. But you do have to do it. Don't go into corporate workplaces thinking you'll just do a good job and you'll succeed. You want to make sure that you connect with people in the best way possible, which is just one of the key tenets of life.

Think of it this way. Every workday, you're taking in communications of all kinds, including conversations, emails, and messages. The ideal way to look at those communications is simply as raw data. And raw data has to be analyzed in order to determine what it really means. It's necessary to decode those communications and understand what's lurking beneath what's being said on the surface. For example, people could be nodding and agreeing with what you say, but, if you know them well enough, you may be able to discern that they're not on board with what you're proposing. They may be avoiding eye contact. They may have their arms crossed in a defensive stance. These kinds of behaviors may or may not indicate disagreement, but you'll know if you've studied them long enough because you'll be able to translate what's *not* being said.

🔒 UNSPOKEN RULE:

What's not said is often more important than what is said.

My team often says I have a sixth sense if a client is not happy, based on how they respond (or don't respond) to emails or the types of things they say (and don't say) in meetings. I don't know if it's a sixth sense, but I do know I look out for meaningful patterns in how people communicate. Here's a story I like to tell that illustrates the kind of experience many have when they realize things aren't the way they're told they are.

It happened a few years ago when I was engaged to work with a client's team. It was 2020, and a part of me felt that they just wanted me, a Black woman, because they thought they needed some outreach at the time. I was OK with it because I knew these people and had worked with them before. I also felt they liked and trusted me, but it turned out they weren't very thoughtful about how I could contribute to the company. There didn't seem to be a serious role for me in their eyes.

So, there were tensions. I learned to recognize whenever there was an issue because the CEO or some other team member would email me and ask if I had time to get on a quick call. That "quick call" prompt was a danger sign that there was going to be bad news involved, because, when they wanted to communicate something positive, they would do it through email. These and other patterns became very apparent, as they are in most workplaces. Certain behaviors signal certain things.

At one point, there was a short period of time when I was completely overloaded. My mom back in North Carolina had surgery and needed me to help out. I had a book coming out that I had to launch, and I needed to talk to the dean of my school over an important matter. In the middle of all this, I was expected to attend a meeting with this client's team—a meeting I had to fly eight hundred miles to attend.

Because of my overstuffed schedule as well as the dean's, it turned out we could only talk on a phone call in the middle of that meeting, which meant I would have to step out to take the call during lunch. The team generally insisted on everyone staying in the meeting when we all got together. Still, I had seen exceptions made for others who had to step out for one reason or another, including having to leave early to pick up their kids or take an important client call. Nonetheless, I was nervous about telling them my situation. Weeks in advance, I overcommunicated all the reasons why I would need to take this call. Not that they reacted as though this was all too much—they just indicated that all was well, and it was no big deal to step out of the meeting for a few minutes. And that is what I did. I never heard another word about it, until, right before our next scheduled meeting, I was asked to hop on a "quick call."

On that "quick call," I was told that I didn't seem engaged at the last meeting and that I seemed distracted. I felt like I was being held to a different standard than everyone else. I intuitively knew this "quick call" was the beginning of the end, but I decided to learn from it. I began taking notes to track what was happening between them and me.

When the next meeting was scheduled, it was on a day that I would be in Italy for work. In the email, they said (as they always did) that if someone couldn't make it, we should let them know, and they would reschedule the meeting. So, I emailed them back that I wouldn't physically be in the country that day.

No response.

This is an organization that prides itself on rapid responses, so it wasn't hard to see where this was going. I reached out two or three more times. Nothing. Nada. Zip. Then, a few weeks later, I got another email saying—guess what—the CEO wanted to hop on a "quick call" with me. He ended up telling me they were going in a "different direction, and since my contract with the company was up anyway.

I pushed back a little. Why didn't they respond to my request to reschedule? Was that last meeting the problem? They just kept repeating that they were going in a different direction. I asked some of the others if that different direction meant other people on the team were being dismissed. They were vague. They said they didn't know.

They knew. It was just me who was suddenly missing from the picture.

Ironically, I had read the room perfectly to the point where I knew when I was going to be shut out of it. I could see where they took advantage of the one time I showed up with less than 100 percent, regardless of my many valid reasons, and used it as an excuse for dismissing me. I wasn't surprised or disappointed because I was completely prepared for the outcome. And I gained some knowledge that made me better able to handle that type of situation in the future.

Learning to read the room helps you be more prepared, less surprised, more action oriented, and less emotional. It allows you to make more informed decisions that reflect the reality of the situation. It also helps you cope with a negative outcome. I wasn't upset when I lost that client because I saw the writing on the wall. Reflecting on the situation, I'd given my very best at the time. If I hadn't, it would have been a different story.

Power in the Workplace

Clearly, in the situation I just described, I had the least amount of power. That, of course, limited my options. All I could do was explain myself, which only seemed to deepen the hole I found myself in. That's why you can't really have a conversation about reading the room without first understanding and accepting the role of power in an organization.

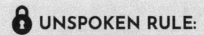

🔒 UNSPOKEN RULE:

"Doing your job" only gets you so far.

Power is often seen as a bad thing. In politics, it can signify corruption. In an organization, power can be linked to people being able to get away with bad behavior, simply because they have some degree of authority. That's why, when I started, power wasn't something I intended to seek. I just wanted to come and do my job. I had yet to learn the unspoken rule that doing your job only gets you so far. You also have to be strategic with your relationships. Otherwise, you will reach a point where your career may stall. I interviewed marketing and creative director Mark El-Rays, who offered some valuable insights into why work relationships can be just as important as your performance:

I believe after you reach a certain level of income, it stops being about what you know, and it starts being about who you know. That can be a challenge if you're not within the power circle, with the people who are able to get you where you need to be. Your skill set only gets you to a certain point, and beyond that, everyone is qualified in some way or another. It starts to become about who is able to introduce you and get you in the door. It takes extra effort to spend time with people like that, get to know them and build those relationships. I challenge myself to do it, because I still feel a bit more at home with the "others" of the world. I know that's an internal bias which can limit me, so I've worked on it.

Bud Bilanich, a business professor at the University of Denver and author of *Climbing the Corporate Ladder*, says too many people believe hard work alone will open the doors. Research backs him up on this. A CNBC/SurveyMonkey Workplace Happiness Survey showed that most workers believed hard work was the key to success.[84] But Bilanich doesn't believe that to be the case: "Everybody's working hard. Everybody's becoming an excellent performer. Working hard ... isn't going to be enough because your competition is also working hard and making contributions. Beyond hard work, the idea that your work has really produced some good, solid, measurable results for your company, is like the price of admission."[85]

Networking is the real key to success once you've reached a certain stage of your career.[86] In our next chapter, we'll talk more specifically about how to build your professional network of influence. For now, consider that power by itself doesn't have to be a bad thing. After all, it is a natural part of organizational dynamics, and just because it's being used doesn't mean it's toward less-than-admirable ends. Power can be used for good—for example, to help other people who may need support or just to improve performance and processes. Once you accept that, there's no need to run from power. The challenge is how to use it wisely and, again, strategically.

I teach a Power and Influence workshop for women because many fear being considered powerful,[87] which goes against stereotypical norms. There are also people with other nondominant identities who feel uncomfortable exercising some authority as they feel they might be too visible. But you do have to be seen, and you do have to be strategic about your workplace relationships. If you do what you're supposed to, there's no guarantee you will be recognized for it. That's why you want to find ways to let people know what you're achieving and how you're meeting (and hopefully exceeding) the organization's expectations and needs.

You also want to try to untangle conflicts when they crop up. Your boss, for example, may treat one of your coworkers a lot better than you—it's like they've picked a favorite, and it isn't you. That can be demoralizing, but a confrontation won't solve anything. It's more productive for you to try to unpack why the boss favors that other person over you. Maybe they focus on ways to make the boss look good, and the boss loves that. A little later in this chapter, you'll see the various ways people acquire power in an organization, and that can give you some insight into why some people at your workplace prosper while others don't. I encourage you to take notes as I did in the situation I related to earlier in the chapter so that you can keep track of any negative patterns that seem to be aimed at you. Again, don't be confrontational when dealing with these kinds of patterns. Instead, ask questions as if trying to gain information about why something is happening. That's how you let them know that you know without turning it into a hot-button issue.

Finally, another great way to acquire some power is to borrow it from someone else. By that, I mean affiliate yourself with a mentor who is influential in your organization. We will get more into this later, but having a higher-up willing to help you navigate your workspace can be invaluable to your career, in terms of both helping you develop the skills necessary to advance in your organization and serving as your booster to other authority figures.

Formal and Informal Power Dynamics

When it comes to reading the room, the first thing to understand is that formal and informal power dynamics are at play.

Formal power is based on role and position. The CEO has tons of formal power as anyone in a C-suite does. But others may also possess informal power that gives them influence in the organization. If someone in a lower position has the trust and confidence of a top executive, for example, that someone could have the ability to talk the executive into doing what they want them to do, especially if that executive has trouble making decisions. An assistant to a high-powered authority figure also gains power simply by controlling access to that authority figure—that type of gatekeeper often gets flooded with compliments by those who want that access.

> 🔒 **UNSPOKEN RULE:**
>
> Power in the workplace goes beyond titles; it's also about access, resources, and relationships that allow you to get things done.

Here is what one anonymous senior vice president in the lending industry says about how power dynamics work at a corporation: "Most of us in this room have thousands of people we are accountable for stretched across the globe. It's impossible to manage or even know what's going on in the depths of the organization. I mean, each of us can fool ourselves into thinking we're smart and running a tight ship. But really the best we can do is create a context and hope that things emerge in a positive way."[88]

That's why, in a *Harvard Business Review* article, author N. Chhaya advocates for employees to note the company's official organizational chart and dig deeper to uncover the hidden organizational chart of networks that actually get the work done regardless of hierarchy.[89] Power is never evenly distributed, nor is it dependent on what's put on paper. Power is always relative, fluid, and changing. For example, on a macro level, labor unions had an enormous amount of power in America throughout the mid-twentieth century. Then, after the Reagan administration, that power waned as corporations consolidated their control and globalization diminished the workers' influence. In recent years, the pendulum has swung back with major strikes by healthcare workers, auto workers, and even the Hollywood creative guilds that have been game changers.

Social psychologists John French and Bertram Raven studied the bases of power in 1959 and came up with six of them.[90,91] Knowing these bases helps you understand how others gain influence and how you can expand yours. Not all these power bases are positive, but they are effective. They are as follows.

LEGITIMATE

Legitimate power comes from occupying a position of authority or from a set of formal relationships. When someone is in a senior position at a company, people serving under them will feel they have to carry out their orders. This kind of power often relies on the person retaining their official role. They can quickly lose power and influence when they are no longer in that role.

REWARD

You've heard of the carrot and the stick? That's what the power of reward is all about—promising a benefit if someone performs. That's the carrot part; the stick part is the threat of punishment (more on that later). For example, if you're promised a bonus for completing a tough assignment, that's reward power. Unfortunately, its influence can be short-lived. Often, once someone actually receives the reward, the incentive is removed, and the power decreases.

EXPERT

Expert power can be leveraged by an individual with above-average skill, competence, and experience. Others lean on these types of people when there's a problem or crisis, which boosts their influence in an organization. This power is independent of someone's position within a company, but it only lasts as long as that expert contributes something substantial and isn't just about gaining personal power.

REFERENT

If you've heard the expression, "You can catch more flies with honey than with vinegar," you already understand referent power, which is based on attracting followers through being liked and respected. Elements that can play into this power include someone's perceived value, worth, or attractiveness. Like expert power, referent power is a highly personal power base and usually not linked to position (although referent power can boost an individual's chances of advancement).

COERCIVE

This is a negative power base, as it involves forcing someone to do something against their will. The coercing person might be in a position where they can punish the other person if they don't comply—the stick part of the "carrot and stick" mentioned in Power Base 2. There are a lot of drawbacks to this approach. It usually leads to a minimum of effort from the other party to only avoid punishment and resentment. This is the type of power where, if it's heavily abused, it may motivate people to leave.

INFORMATIONAL

When you can control the flow of data and have access to confidential information and/or secret sources, you have informational power because you know things others don't. In this day and age, that can be an awesome source of power, but it only lasts while you have that kind of access.

Whenever someone seems to have excessive power relative to their position, try to determine which of these power bases they're working from. This will give you more insight into the power dynamics. Also, think about your own power base. What about you is going to provide you with influence in the workplace? How can you tap into it?

Know Your Audience

One of the obstacles to reading the room clearly and objectively just might be you. All of us have prejudices and biases. We all have blind spots that prevent us from seeing the whole picture. And yes, all of us go through difficult times. These factors can prevent us from thinking clearly and making false assumptions about others, so we need to open our minds and use our empathy to find common ground. We sometimes need to cut people a break like we do for ourselves.

Let's say your manager is just returning from paternity leave and is worried about resuming their position and performance levels. That person might be a little irritable and abrupt with you in a meeting. Now, you can take that kind of interchange personally or step back and say to yourself, "Wow, he's under a lot of stress. I should try to find a way to help him get back on track." In this case, the latter is the better choice. Of course, if there is a never-ending succession of rude behaviors, that's a very different story. But, in a case like this, you again have to look at what this person is *not* saying because they may not feel comfortable admitting they're struggling. Instead of being offended, if you can figure out the underlying issue and be a part of the solution, it's better for them, you, and the team. Yes, there are bad people out there. But it's helpful to give everyone a chance while being cautious at the same time. People always reveal their true colors over time, and trust you'll see them when they do. But until you're sure, avoid creating conflicts and show them a modicum of trust.

Knowing your audience can decode some of your workplace's most important unspoken rules. Gary Smith, co-founder and senior partner of Ivy Planning Group consulting firm, puts it this way:

When I think about unspoken rules, it's the way decision "ties" should be broken. I'll give you a simple example. It's the end of day, and you have two calls come in at the exact same time. One is from a customer, and one is from your boss. You only have time to call one because you are about to jump on an airplane. Which call are you supposed to return? Well, the unspoken rule is, that's going to depend on the company. It might depend on the boss you work for. But it would be nice to know which call I'm supposed to return. Are we a customer-focused organization so I always call the customer? Or is it the standard that around here, if your boss calls, you better call your boss back?

You can almost always build positive and productive relationships if you prioritize them. But it takes a willingness to accept everyone else's humanity and an understanding that this is not a black-and-white world. News flash: people are not perfect, and that includes you. Recognize that *all* humans are cognitively biased in one way or another. As an individual, the more you are aware of these biases, the more you can help thwart their negative impact.

Here are a few more common workplace biases you may encounter and how to strategically deal with them.

RECENCY BIAS/AVAILABILITY BIAS

This bias boils down to the question posed by the title of an old Janet Jackson song, "What Have You Done for Me Lately." Sometimes, your manager will be obsessed with only the most recent results, especially if they've been disappointing. What you should do in this instance is not wait for that annual review. Share your progress and accomplishments with your manager throughout the year (quarterly is a good option). Putting it in writing will help them recall this information at performance review time.[92]

HALO/HORNS EFFECT

You've probably been told that making a good first impression at various instances throughout your life is essential. This bias confirms that importance. When someone immediately judges you at your first meeting, and it's not a favorable judgment, that can be a roadblock in your relationship. You could end up feeling like you're in an inescapable negative cycle with this person. This becomes much more difficult if that person is your manager.

Your best move is to try to disrupt that cycle with data. When it's performance review time, write out your review for your own benefit so that you have specific examples of your achievements and competencies on the top of mind. Be honest about areas of opportunity, and use specific examples and output metrics when possible. Fit what you're doing into the "big picture" of the company goals.

Beyond the performance review, look for opportunities for the manager to see you in a different light through bonding at social events or volunteering for a work project to deepen the relationship. You also might want to avoid being at the mercy of this one individual. Ask for multiple sources of feedback formally if possible or informally if it can't be part of the formal process. At the very least, you'll get a more fair and rounded perspective of how you're doing on the job.[93]

THE SIMILAR-TO-ME EFFECT

When superiors rate their subordinates, the more similar the parties are, the higher the rating the superior tends to give.[94] We all tend to bond with people we perceive to be "like us." The problem comes when your manager *isn't* like you and lets it impact their assessment of you. This plays into another common human unconscious bias, the desire to create a "mini-me," someone who shares their likes and/ or beliefs or feels close to because the other person is of a similar age, experience base, gender, or race.[95,96]

Find a way to connect beyond the superficial because people generally have more in common with others than they think. So, find out what your manager's interests are and find new ways to bond. Things like food, music, and sports are generally easy but authentic connection points. You might also want to focus on a skill or a part of the job you can learn from your manager and ask to shadow them. This way, you create an area of opportunity and increase your connection with your boss. Besides, you and your managers and coworkers automatically have something in common. You have the same employer as well as the same goals in the workplace.[97]

Things to Remember

1. When reading the room, analyze situations based on what is said and what's not said. Look for recurring communication patterns so you can flag negative situations and lean into positive ones.

2. Understand the various sources of power that people draw from to increase their authority. Analyze them, and leverage them for your advancement.

3. Use distance and objectivity when you size up other people. Be aware of common biases both in them and work to minimize your natural blind spots.

CHAPTER EXERCISE: FIGURE OUT THE POWER DYNAMICS

In this chapter, I share examples of how formal and informal power dynamics can impact your success at work. It is important to understand the power dynamics in your department and organization. Here are some questions to answer:

1. Who holds authority in your organization? Look beyond job titles to see who the decision-makers with impact are.

   _____

   _____

2. Observe who exercises different modes of power[98], for example:

   □ Who do others seek out for information[99] (information power)

   _____

   _____

   □ Who always get approval for additional resources (reward power)

   _____

   _____

   □ Who is well-known and liked (referent power)

   _____

   _____

3. Question whether there have been situational shifts in power. In certain situations, relational power can trump hierarchical power.[100]

   _____

   _____

Reflecting on these questions can help you read the room and strategically expand your network of influence, which we explore in the next chapter.

NOTES ON POWER DYNAMICS

What are some Unspoken Rules on power dynamics in your industry or specific workplace? (This is a good question to ask a peer or mentor if you are unsure)

_____

_____

_____

_____

_____

_____

_____

_____

_____

_____

_____

CHAPTER SIX

Expand Your Networks
of Influence

If you want 1 year of prosperity, grow grain.
If you want 10 years of prosperity, grow trees.
If you want 100 years of prosperity, grow people.

—CHINESE PROVERB

An old African proverb says, "If you want to go fast, go alone; if you want to go far, go together."

Most of what we've been talking about thus far is about going it alone by understanding the unspoken rules so that you can tap into, present, and leverage your best self in the workplace. This is good, but at the same time, it can be a bit limiting. You may not want to stay in your current job forever. You may want to work at a different company. You may want to change direction or even your entire career. And even if your goal is to stay right where you are, you want to have the best possible experience and get the most out of it. Your best bet in accomplishing any of these goals is to build relevant relationships with people who can give you the advice, encouragement, and opportunities you seek.

You can only go so far alone. But with the right network, your future can be unlimited. This chapter will help you build that network and give you the cheat codes that will allow you to expand your circle of influence beyond your current friends and coworkers. The first step is having the right mindset.

Getting Past Your Fear

There are two types of folks: those comfortable reaching out to people they don't know and those who aren't. And being the second type, the shy type, can have consequences.

How widespread is this problem? As an example, you'd imagine someone hired to be a B2B salesperson would be OK with cold-calling potential customers, right? After all, their job might depend on that ability. And yet, a study found that 48 percent of salespeople were actively afraid to do so![101]

If virtually half of a sales force sweats out cold-calling, then the psychological challenge of trying to connect with people we don't know must be formidable indeed—which is why your first obstacle to expanding your sphere of influence may be your hesitation to reach out to someone you don't know. It's far easier to sink back into your comfort zone and keep talking to people you already have a positive relationship with. But that tends to limit your horizons.

So why are we so frightened to reach out? Well, let's go back to the study of B2B salespeople, who provided two clear reasons for being anxious about cold calling: (1) they were afraid of sounding like a salesperson and (2) they were afraid of being rejected. Broaden the emotions expressed in those reasons, and they can easily apply to all of us. In the first case, we're looking for professional help, and we don't want the other person to think we're trying to use them. Research shows that professional networking can lead to feelings of "dirtiness," particularly for people with lower power in an organization.[102] The more self-serving the networking feels, the more discomfort people tend to have, especially when the experience feels forced instead of spontaneous.

In the second case of fear of rejection, well, we don't really have to expand on that. Nobody wants to be turned down, especially when they're trying to connect with someone they respect who may be at a higher professional level than them. But instead of looking at potential rejection, focus on the positive possibilities, and it could be a game changer.

🔒 UNSPOKEN RULE:

If you want something, you must ask for it, even if it's uncomfortable.

When Steve Jobs was only twelve, he looked up the number of HP's co-founder, Bill Hewlett, in the phonebook (for those of you who remember phonebooks). Then he had the nerve to cold-call Hewlett on the pretext of requesting any leftover electronic parts the company might have. The executive was amused Jobs dared to call him up out of the blue and was impressed with the kid's knowledge and drive. Jobs not only got those parts, but he also got his first entry into the tech world. Hewlett offered him an internship at HP, where he ended up on an assembly line, using those same parts to build frequency counters for the company.

"I've always found something to be very true, which is most people don't get those experiences because they never ask," Jobs said in 1994. "I've never found anybody that didn't want to help me if I asked them for help."[103] I emphasize that last part of the quote because that's what you want to focus on—not your fear. Most people do want to help if they can. You just have to be willing to ask.

Jobs went on to say, "You've got to be willing to crash and burn, with people on the phone, with starting a company, with whatever. If you're afraid of failing, you won't get very far." I've made these kinds of connections in the past as have many of my colleagues, including Kimberly Hogg Massey. Kimberly knows firsthand the importance of having the courage to connect and of not taking the outcome personally: "I had a mentor who once told me if you don't ask, then the mistake is just on you. Most people want to help … I always believed that the worst people can say is no."

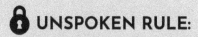

🔒 **UNSPOKEN RULE:**

It's not *what* you know but *who* you know.

Build Relationships across Differences

Being comfortable reaching out to new people is half the battle of expanding your network. However, there is a major blind spot in most social networks because they lack diversity. Being around people who are different from us gives us access to more information and makes us more creative and better decision-makers and problem-solvers.[104]

Yet, regarding our social and professional networks, we tend to form connections with people with similar attributes to us (race, education, social status, etc.).[105] For example, 75 percent of white Americans say their social network is almost entirely white, 65 percent of Black Americans report their network is almost entirely Black, and 46 percent of Hispanic Americans say their network is entirely Hispanic.[106] Beyond race, one in five Americans say they seldom or never interact with someone who does not share their religion (22 percent), political party (23 percent), or sexual orientation (31 percent). Looking globally, in the United Kingdom, 22 percent of people said everyone in their network had a similar education level, 39 percent had the same ethnic group, and 28 percent had the same religion.[107]

Intentionally building relationships across differences can be a game changer in the workplace. Janet Smith, the co-founder and president of the IVY Planning Group consulting firm, shared this observation:

As a consultant there are many times when our engagement is confidential, and we get to see salaries and bonuses. It's disheartening when I see pay inequities. I will see a Black or Latino middle manager who's walking around with their chest puffed out because they think they are doing well, and I wish I could tell them, "You've been paid 20 percent less than your colleague, and you don't even know it." I wish they would talk to other people, not just other Black and Brown people but also build relationships across differences. The white man who is talking to another white man is also likely to talk to you if you build a relationship with him. We may not want to do it, but it's so critical that we build relationships across differences.

It's important to have a variety of perspectives to tap into, even if you may not agree. You will still learn from one another and better understand their viewpoint. You don't just want cheerleaders who will praise your every move. You may want someone who's not that fond of you to give you honest feedback.

Obviously, if that feedback is dishonest or abusive, you don't go back to that well a second time, but what you might get is a very valuable reality check that will help you grow. President Bill Clinton was known to be one of the best debaters of his time, not because he was so much smarter than everyone but because he was also gifted at understanding the opposition's perspective.[108] With that in mind, get out of your own mental box, and expose yourself to other ways of thinking.

Human Connection in a Remote World

Since COVID-19, remote and hybrid working has become the new normal, with 80 percent of global organizations allowing some level of remote and hybrid working.[109] By 2025, it is estimated that 22 percent of Americans[110] will be working remotely. These trends are expected to continue to increase; globally, 35 percent of organizations already allow employees to work remotely from other countries.[111] The changes in the workplace landscape necessitate thinking about expanding our networks differently. In remote situations, people cannot rely on spontaneous opportunities to connect, such as in the elevator or water cooler. However, networking becomes even more critical for building social connections, developing internal support networks, and learning firm and industry insights and overall professional development.

Then there is the challenge of proximity bias, which can lead to inequities between collated and remote employees, such as remote workers getting promoted less often than their peers despite being 15 percent more productive on average.[112] Being strategic about your networks of influence has become even more critical for success in today's remote workplace.

Identity has an impact here, too. In my research in partnership with Future Forum, we found that women, working mothers, and people of color were more likely to want to work remotely than white men, primarily because they experienced fewer microaggressions and feelings of exclusion working from home.[113] The remote workplace can be especially challenging for these demographics as they are at higher risk of becoming isolated and are often reached out to less for relationship building.[114]

Making human connections is critical for expanding your network, especially in a remote world. Networking strategies such as periodic outreach to reconnect, engaging in ERGs, and participating in virtual learning communities can help employees stay connected and visible. Further, proactively looking for opportunities to engage in meaningful experiences is critical, particularly for people with non-dominant identities. The more people get to know you, the deeper the connections and, thus, the stronger your network. However, sometimes, we miss these opportunities right in front of us. As Janet Smith remembers:

I was coaching a new chief diversity officer, and it was a stretch opportunity for them at a new company. The CEO asked them to go to a black-tie evening event where they would be representing the company along with a few other executives. They asked me, "Do I have to go?" And I said, "Are you kidding me? Do you have to go, no you WANT to go!" They replied, "Well, you know, they didn't talk about this when they were talking to me about the job. I mean, do I get paid overtime for this?"

So I said, "Let's take a step back. You have a salary job. It's no longer about the hours you put in. It's a privilege to be hired not just for your skills but for your potential. To step up as an executive, you should accept this gift of time with the CEO. After hours with other C-suite leaders is an opportunity to represent your company. Now you have the privilege of being asked to build your relationship with the leadership team. Jump on it! If you need a babysitter, go hire one. Someone has to teach us these unspoken rules.

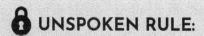 **UNSPOKEN RULE:**

Embracing invitations to build connections can unlock opportunities.

Join the Club

Diversifying and expanding your professional network is a pivotal aspect of career growth, and a highly effective avenue to achieve this is by actively participating in a professional association or industry group. By becoming a member of such organizations, you not only engage with like-minded professionals within your field but also connect with individuals who align with and represent your career objectives and aspirations. This strategic involvement provides a platform for networking, knowledge exchange, and collaborative opportunities, fostering meaningful connections that can contribute significantly to your professional development and success. As a *Forbes* article put it, "[O]ne of the best ways that you can remain career-relevant, marketable and valuable in today's environment is to join and become active in a professional association."[115]

These types of organizations represent almost every industry or profession you can imagine—including ones based on geographic or ethnic commonalities. One in particular, the PhD Project, was essential for me at the beginning of my professional journey. The PhD Project was founded in 1994 to diversify corporate America by diversifying the role models in the front of classrooms. Their results[116] over the last three decades are inspiring. Because of this Project:

- it more than sextupled the number of historically underrepresented business professors in the United States, from 294 in 1994 to over 1,700 today;

- approximately three hundred diverse doctoral students are receiving help to pursue their academic careers; and

- an immeasurable number of students have benefited from the teaching, mentoring, and guiding of the Project professors.

A mentor suggested I attend a PhD Project conference when I was a senior in college and said that it would be good for me to see what the Project had to offer in terms of guiding me toward my goals.

At the conference, I attended many panels with people sharing their academic and professional experiences. I talked to current graduate students and professors, which helped demystify the process of getting a PhD in business and helped me decide to move in that direction. The conference gave me my own cheat code regarding how I would approach graduate school, as it does for so many others. The PhD Project is special and is structured to function like a community. If you are admitted into a business school PhD program, you then become a part of the cohort in your area for the Project. I became a part of the management cohort, and every summer while I was in grad school, they paid for me to attend the Academy of Management conference.

Because the conference is so massive, they bring you in a few days beforehand for a preconference, featuring panels, discussions, dinners, and networking opportunities. You get to network with tenured professors at big-name schools and doctoral students across the country pursuing similar PhDs. Many of these people become your future colleagues.

I met some of my very best friends through the PhD Project. Every year I go back to it, it feels like a family reunion as I reconnect with people who are now on the other side of their doctoral program and many of them on the other side of tenure.

Here's a good example of the relationships that can happen with this kind of networking group. I met my now-close friend Alison at the Project. At the time, she was in the same year as me in her doctoral program at Tulane, and we were both about to enter our comprehensive exams, which I was struggling to study for. Even though we had just met, and she was all the way down in New Orleans while I was up in Chicago, we decided to become accountability partners. We would check in weekly via text and chat to see whether we were sticking to our studying benchmarks. I made another friend, Erika, who was a year ahead of me, and we also formed a deep connection. As a matter of fact, I'm now the godmother to her two children.

In short, through the PhD Project, I found a circle of people I could trust and lean on when I needed advice and help. Looking back, I realized I should have leaned on them more. But I got in my own way. At the time, a professor who wasn't part of the Project told me if I wasn't going to go for a job in academia, I shouldn't tell anybody else because I might not be able to graduate. I believe he was trying to look out for me, but the result was I didn't tell anyone about the postgrad school plans I was struggling with. I know now that they would have helped me navigate the situation without judgment. It was another case where I was afraid to ask for help—and could have used it.

Despite my unconventional career choices, the relationships I started with people mattered to me because I felt a sense of care from them. Even after several years, they still cheer me on, which taught me a valuable lesson to trust the relationships I have built. Yes, they encouraged me, but I could have had more support if I had asked for it. Instead, I felt very alone and didn't feel like I could talk to any of the professors at my school.

Fast-forward to last year's Project PhD conference. Someone there that I was mentoring told me she, like me, was thinking of leaving academia and pursuing a career like mine. Because of my experience, I knew exactly what to tell her. I gave her a list of names to talk to, the same people I wish I had talked to back in the day. Unlike me, she went ahead and approached them and ended up deciding to stay in academia. Still, she made an informed decision based on her conversations with these other mentors. I was glad I could open those doors for her, but I still wished I had done the same thing for myself.

So, seek out a group like the PhD Project that suits your needs and goals. And, unlike me in the early days, lean into it. If you don't ask for help when needed, you're doing yourself a disservice.

Mentors and Sponsors

When considering the span of your influence, mentors and sponsors play critical roles. A mentor will freely share their knowledge and provide guidance to a less-experienced individual. You can find them inside or outside your organization, depending on their experience and expertise. Anyone who has support and advice to share can provide effective mentorship, regardless of their current role.

On the contrary, sponsors are usually in a position of power and will actively promote your professional growth as well as provide access to opportunities at work and advocate for the career advancement of a less-experienced individual. As Gallup puts it, "A sponsor opens the door to opportunities for another employee, while a mentor supports and guides an employee so that they can open the door for themselves."[117] Another difference? Usually, a sponsor will choose you when they recognize something special about you. In contrast, you will usually choose your own mentors. You might even seek out someone you don't know personally for that role in your life.

Let me share how I connected with someone who turned out to be a very important mentor. Dr. Laura Morgan Roberts is an organizational psychologist, professor, author, and keynote speaker. When I was in college, Laura came to my campus as a guest lecturer for our psychology lab. I was impressed with her bio and felt like she was the perfect role model for me. So, after her talk, I approached her and asked if I could walk her to her car. I knew she was very busy, so I didn't want to take up too much of her time. Walking with her was a great way to get some exclusive face time with her, and I've used this strategy more than once to connect with busy executives.

During our parking lot chat, I asked Laura if she would be open to me being her research assistant. She agreed, and four months later, I needed an advisor for a fellowship, and she agreed to do that for me as well! We quickly formed a working relationship, and she became an important mentor. She even wrote a letter of recommendation to help get me into grad school at Northwestern. When I went there, it turned out her sister lived in Chicago, and every time Laura came to visit, we would grab lunch, and she would give me more valuable advice.

I even ended up babysitting her kids. My first *Harvard Business Review* article was in collaboration with her almost fifteen years after we met. Throughout my career, Laura has continued to be a cherished mentor and friend. That's the kind of meaningful relationship that can spring from something as simple and short as walking someone to their car.

Of course, that kind of opportunity might not present itself to you. There may be a person you're interested in having as a mentor, but they may be in another state or country. How do you make the connection? Usually, this is going to be a person in a higher position who is probably already overscheduled and overburdened. So, the last thing you want to do is add another responsibility to their overflowing to-do list.

I know this firsthand because every so often, I get an email from someone just flat out asking, "Will you be my mentor?" Often, I don't have the bandwidth to build a meaningful connection based on that email alone. Instead, keep this idea in mind. If you want someone to help you, offer something helpful for them. I told you about how

I asked Laura if I could be her research assistant. To her, that was me lightening her load, not throwing more weight. So now I had a receptive audience.

If you contact a desired mentor, begin by letting them know you'd love to work with them in some capacity. When I get that kind of email, I respond quickly, even when I don't have anything for them to do at the moment. I still want to honor that attitude and offer encouragement.

It can be more challenging to establish this kind of connection with a potential sponsor, as they are usually two or three levels up from you, while a mentor can be a peer—for example, someone who's been with the organization longer than you and can give you some guidance. Again, sponsors will usually recognize you. Maybe you nailed a presentation, and they happen to be in the room and give you a boost within the organization. I spoke with Juliet Hall, an award-winning author of *Own Your Opportunities*, speaker, and coach, to get her take on sponsors, and she said:

What I would encourage people to do is focus on mentorship versus sponsorship. I just have this belief that you choose your mentors, but your sponsors choose you. I'm a big tennis fan, so I always go to Venus and Serena Williams as my examples. They had to prove themselves and get some wins under their belts before they could get sponsors. They were unknowns, and it wasn't until they established themselves that it changed. So don't just think that after the first month or even the first year of working for an organization that you can just automatically get a sponsor. Why would somebody sponsor you if they don't know you? If nobody is talking about you? So, demonstrate your value first. Show up on time, do what you say you're going to do, show that you are a contributor, and make sure that you have a track record of follow-through.

Also, know that one mentor cannot meet all your needs. In my interview with Nzinga Shaw, she articulates how she seeks out a variety of mentors and how she ensures she's chosen the right ones:

I never sought out mentors for the sake of having a mentor. I always sought out mentors with intention. I have different mentors in my life right now. The women that mentored me about motherhood are moms. I'm not asking women without kids for advice on child-rearing, because they can't give me advice on child-rearing. Mentors should be people who are expert enough to give you concrete advice on what you need to know about. In the workplace, if I'm looking to break into the revenue-generating side of the business, I don't want a mentor on the side of the business that costs the company money, like HR. I'm going to go to the revenue generators and ask someone to help shepherd me. You have to seek out real expertise and mentorship skills, before just allowing a person to take up your time with advice that may not serve you well.

You should make your mentor relationships a two-way street. You may think there's nothing you can do for your mentor, but there is such a thing as reverse mentoring. Your perspective as a younger person can be helpful, just in terms of advising them about trends or technology they may not fully understand. So, ask them questions like, "What do you have going on? How can I support you? Can I be helpful in any way?"

Sometimes you can serve as a resource for them or even just a sounding board. I used to always think of colleagues more senior than me as not needing anything. But over the years, I've found that not to be true. Give back to those giving to you, and go beyond surface questions like, "How can I help you?" Dig deeper into specifics, and offer to help if they are facing any obstacles or need someone to give an assist. If you can provide a solution for a mentor, it increases your bond and their trust in you.

Finally, if you need extra help staying accountable or achieving specific goals, you may benefit from adding a trained coach to your "roster" of mentors. Not only will a coach keep you motivated and focused, but a good coach will also provide specific, tailored guidance designed to help you overcome obstacles and grow into your full potential.

Your Personal Board of Directors

A one-on-one mentor only has so much expertise and experience to share with you; sometimes, that's not enough. We tend to pick mentors who are or were in our field, which makes perfect sense. Who better to guide us in that career? But there are times when we need different kinds of advice from different perspectives. This is why it will benefit you to build a diverse network of individuals, more popularly known these days as a personal board of directors.[118]

First, understand that having a personal board of directors is different from having multiple mentors. Mentors will spend a significant amount of time working with you. Everyone on your personal board of directors, however, will merely be independent advisers. As the *Harvard Business Review* describes, "Just as a company looks to its board for guidance, these people are there to offer you support in a broader sense. Each director usually specializes in a different area: a great manager, a skilled writer, a savvy freelancer, a wise parent, a compassionate friend, a talented peer, and so on. As such, each is able to offer you advice specific to their expertise."[119]

Generally, you will be making much smaller asks to someone on your board of directors than you would with a mentor or sponsor. For example, if you have a tax question, you might text it to a financial expert who can answer it for you instantly. That only takes both of you a minute. You may also want to have individuals in your network who are in a different field than you are at the moment—a field you might be interested in pivoting to, for example.

This process of putting together your board of directors will be largely informal. First, you have to think about your long-term and short-term goals. Then, think about who you might need to consult with along the way if you're going to reach those goals. Which professionals doing similar or different work can you connect with? What sponsors might you need? What experts? Who are the thought leaders you need to align yourself alongside?

You want to be intentional about who you have on your board of directors. While you will meet many of them naturally throughout your life, there are others you will need to make an effort to connect with. And you don't want to wait until you need something to call on them. You probably won't get far if you don't know them that well or even at all. Instead, you want to try to build authentic relationships *before* needing them.

Whichever way you start one of these relationships, it is important to keep it going. In my interview with Mark El-Rayes, he put it like this: "What I would have told the me of fifteen years ago is the importance of maintaining relationships. I think there are people in my life who got to where I would have wanted to go and I was working with them at the time when they started—if I had kept that relationship, I would have grown right alongside of them."

Mark is absolutely correct that keeping up with people who impress you can be a blessing. Jenga is someone I met when she was an undergrad, and we were both in the same sorority. After we graduated, we stayed in touch, and I shared my career goals. She ended up with my dream job at a Big 4 consulting firm. When I was ready to leave graduate school, I asked her for a letter of recommendation. That's when I discovered she was about to leave the firm and my dream job was about to open up. I didn't have to ask. She flat out told me she had put my name into the mix for the role. I went through the interview process, and I not only got the job, but Jenga was also able to tell me the reasons why she left—important inside information that would help me avoid the same difficult situations that led her to find another position.

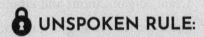

🔒 UNSPOKEN RULE:

Inside information is valuable information.

Finally, I want to stress again that you should be intentional in choosing your board of directors. Make a list of the missing pieces, and actively seek out people to fill them. Say you want to work at Amazon in a few years. Well, if you go to a conference and you encounter someone from Amazon, try to connect. How? Yes, networking can be uncomfortable if you're not used to doing it.

But you must keep in mind that you have been networking your entire life—by making friends, interacting with teachers and other authority figures, and asking family members for help and advice. So, pinpoint the same kinds of techniques that brought you success in those situations and see if they translate to a more professional setting.

Here are three suggested activities to helping you initiate, build, and deepen your existing network:[120]

USE YOUR ELEVATOR PITCH

At the end of chapter 1, I suggested crafting an elevator pitch so that you could immediately and concisely communicate who you are, what you're about, and what you're after. When you network, use that elevator pitch to quickly connect with people and start a conversation. Think about meaningful parts of your background you would like to share, and also show interest in the other person and their story.

BUILD A COMPANY-CONNECTION FINDER

Compile a list of "dream" organizations and employers you're interested in working for, and use it to strategize how you might be able to network with those entities. Start by identifying potential connections you might have with them. You can use resources like LinkedIn or Alumni Advisors Hub. From there, find positions at these organizations that might be of interest to you. Take time to review the types of open positions, the qualifications needed, and how interested in them you might be. This will also motivate you to think about what your focus should be in terms of growing your specific network in the right direction.

DEEPEN YOUR CONNECTIONS TO CREATE YOUR BOARD OF DIRECTORS

Your board of directors can include peers, friends, family members, colleagues, or leaders whom you can reach out to for advice, guidance, and feedback. Look for people who:

- will celebrate you,

- validate your feelings,

- will be an advocate for you,

- will give you honest feedback,

- hold you accountable,

- will mentor you,

- share knowledge,

- challenge you to go bigger,

- have more experience than you,

- are a great connector,

- have organizational power,

- will help you develop your skills,

- navigate workplace politics well,

- are a leader you admire, and

- know the unwritten rules of a company.

Feel free to add or edit this list so that it makes the most sense for you. Make sure you have a diverse group of people. This means not having everyone on your board come from the same industry, organization, or demographic background.

I myself have realized the benefits of maximizing my network of influence. Truly, it was only when I started to fundraise through my nonprofit work that I ever networked at a high level. Like many others, I don't enjoy asking my friends for help. But, when I had to ask for donations to get me to the $30,000 mark for a Juneteenth fundraiser, I pushed myself out of my comfort zone and happily discovered there are great people in my network, and I should be utilizing them.

Nobody does it all alone. That's why networks are so necessary. Just remember networking is a two-way street. Ask what you can do to help the other person too. Realize that you are also bringing something to the table, and even if you can't do anything for the other person at the moment, there may be a time when you can. These are *relationships*, and relationships go both ways.

Things to Remember

- Work on losing your fear of approaching mentors and others you want in your network. Choose opportunities (walking them to their car, taking an elevator ride with them) where you can spend a few minutes alone.

- When you first talk to a potential mentor, start by offering to help them with their work. Lighten their burden; don't add to it by asking them immediately to do something for you.

- Create your board of directors—a group of people with experience in different walks of life who can advise you on different situations. Expand that network to reflect your goals and focus, to help you on your way rather than hold you back.

CHAPTER EXERCISE: MAP YOUR NETWORK

"Network mapping" is a visual representation of all the elements in a network and how they are connected. Usually, it applies to technology, but for our purposes, I'm asking you to create a map of your network, giving you a visual representation of your areas of influence. The goal is to have a diverse and varied group of people in your network so that you can get a multitude of perspectives when you need them. How does your network stack up?

- Take a piece of paper, and divide it into four columns.

- In the first column, write the person's name.

- In the second column, write how you know the person.

- In the third column, write the most important attribute you associate with this person, whether it's what they do, where they do it, what they're an expert in, or whatever reason they matter to you.

- Finally, in the fourth column, write down all the ways this person is different from you—things like race, religious background, socioeconomic status, where they're from, and so forth. Most of us do not have a very diverse network, so look at this as an opportunity for you.

Name/Company Role	Relationship	Most Important Attribute	How are we different?

When you're finished, look at your map. This should give you a clearer picture of who is in your network and where there may be holes you need to fill.

NOTES ON NETWORKING

<u>What Unspoken Rules have you experienced</u>
<u>in networking?</u>

_____

_____

_____

_____

_____

_____

<u>My board of directors:</u>

_____

_____

_____

_____

_____

_____

_____

SECTION THREE

Look forward by moving beyond what's right in front of you.

Develop your own playbook to build a career and a life that fits and nourishes the person you are.

SECTION THREE

CHAPTER SEVEN
Master the ABCs of Negotiation

The most common way people give up their power is by thinking they don't have any.

—ALICE WALKER

Of all the chapters in this book, this one may be my favorite. Not just because I happen to love negotiation (more on that later), but because most of life is a negotiation. I'm not just talking about negotiations over things like salary or when you're buying a car or a house. I'm talking about everyday life.

We all negotiate every day with potential employers, coworkers, roommates, landlords, parents, bosses, merchants, spouses, and service providers. We negotiate to determine what price we will pay, when to check out of a hotel, what movie to watch, and who will clean the kitchen.

Yet even though negotiations are ubiquitous in our everyday lives, many of us know little about the psychology or strategy behind effective negotiation. Why do we sometimes get our way, while other times we walk away feeling frustrated by our inability to get what we want?

Also, why are kids so much better at negotiating than we are? Dr. Meg Myers Morgan, the author of *Everything Is Negotiable*, makes this point brilliantly in a TEDx talk, in which she talks about her four-year-old daughter and how she's the most successful negotiator she knows.

> One of her many, many schemes is to convince us to let her reserve something for later. If we won't let her have it in the moment, she'll ask for a cookie. The answer's no. She'll nod respectfully, ringlets bouncing, and she'll ask for the same thing in a slightly different way. Can she put a cookie on the kitchen table? When we ask why she wants to do that, she says that perhaps later, for being a bit more reasonable, the answer will be yes, and if it is, the cookie will be ready for her. This is surprisingly effective at any given time. In our house, the kitchen table is littered with objects and treats over which my child is in current negotiations, and yet by bedtime, the table is always magically cleared of clutter. She's an example for women everywhere.

Kids are great at negotiating because they approach it with a pure and (mostly) innocent spirit. There's also the fact that, as any parent will tell you, they're relentless when they want something. They never assume "no" is a final answer and are fearless about their requests. After all, why be afraid? Why *not* go after what you want?

But eventually, we all grow up. We learn rules in school and are repeatedly told we can't just get whatever we ask for. We absorb the limitations that are placed on most of us. And maybe we never quite figure out how to negotiate for bigger and more complex goals. At the same time, the negotiations in question become more high stakes. It's one thing to negotiate for a cookie and quite another thing to get an employer to give you what you think you deserve, especially when *you* are not even sure.

Suppose you're uncomfortable with negotiating when it comes to your career. In that case, you could be holding yourself back in several ways—not just the salary you earn but also what position you hold and where you stand when it comes to power dynamics in the workplace. All of these elements are incredibly important, particularly if you have a nondominant identity and feel you walked into your job at a disadvantage from the get-go. In this chapter, we'll work on helping you overcome any hesitation you might feel when negotiating and how to maximize your results from it.

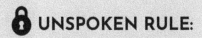

🔒 UNSPOKEN RULE:

Everything is negotiable.

Negotiation Can Happen Almost Anywhere

I'm different from most in that I never lost my appetite for negotiating after I grew up. As a matter of fact, I teach MBA classes on the subject. But I wasn't always a master negotiator. As an adult, I didn't know what I could negotiate and what I couldn't. So, most of my negotiating was done with family and friends. Slowly, I realized that everything was negotiable—meaning there were so many more possibilities than I initially envisioned for myself. Since that time, I have made it a point to figure out precisely how to go after what I wanted in the most powerful ways possible.

I realize not everybody has that kind of drive. Many of my female students, for example, express to me that they are timed to negotiate at work. And I agree, if you're uncomfortable negotiating in any scenario, work may not be the best place to start. I try to shift their mindset to viewing everything as negotiable in some way—and by everything, I mean not just money. Most of us think of negotiating as always being about the numbers (except for those kids who think cookies are currency)—salary amounts, prices, discounts, and so forth. But there's much more to it than that.

Nonsalary negotiable items:

- Start date

- Job title

- Commission percentage

- Travel benefits (i.e., reward points)

- Moving expenses

- Transportation benefits (metro or bus fare)

- Retirement benefits matching

- Phone allowance

- Discounts on company products

- Signing bonus

- Remote work

- Equity compensation

- Office space

- Guaranteed severance package

- Tuition reimbursement

- Day care reimbursement

- Flexible scheduling

- Additional leave[121]

Dr. Charis Chambers laid it out perfectly for me in our interview:

What I found is everything is open to negotiation. Once, I was told management had to approve every speaking engagement for all physicians, and I refused to agree to that. I created my own schedule instead; I said I would work 80 percent here, enough to be full-time, but I'll still be able to take Fridays off and do speaking engagements without asking for permission and without losing patient volume. I came up with a creative solution where everyone could win. If you reframe negotiation in terms of everyone's interests, then the negotiation doesn't have to be so emotional. It can just be mathematical and logical.

I feel as though people really miss the mark by not seeing everything through a negotiation lens. As Dr. Charis said, you can absolutely negotiate rules that don't make sense for you and limitations that are excessive. There are also always moments in your career after the initial job offer where you can negotiate things like job assignments, performance reviews, service work, your job title, your reporting structure, your exit package, and more. Vipula Gandhi explained how she has navigated to negotiate her role and what was best for her organization, where she is the most senior woman.

I've often negotiated for bigger responsibilities. I came to the US. I said, "I want a managing partner position, and here's the reason why I believe I'm deserving of this." I had to ask for it. Nobody came to me and said, "Take this position." First, I pointed out the company had three managing partners in the US, which was a very inefficient way of organizing. It created silos and internal competition. We needed to encourage competition externally, not internally. The company needed a structure where there was one person over the US market, not three managing partners. I raised this point, leadership agreed, and I became US enterprise (managing partner). Two years later I said OK, now you have a single head of the US, but you have this EMEA business running separately. There is no collaboration going on. There are no best practices being shared. You need to put both under one person and guess what, I'm your person. Now I am the global head of enterprise business (managing partner).

🔒 **UNSPOKEN RULE:**

Negotiations can happen at any point in the employee life cycle, not just during hiring.

The ABCs of Negotiation

When I teach negotiation, I break it down into some simple ABC steps:

- **A**wareness and agency
- **B**uilding relationships
- **C**reating clear outcomes

Let's look at them one at a time.

AWARENESS AND AGENCY

Before you can begin to negotiate, you have to be aware of the situation, what's possible in a negotiation, and when the time is right to begin the negotiation. For example, let's say you are negotiating with a new employer on how many days will you be able to work remotely. Let's say the company does not have a standard remote-hybrid policy (which they should). The manager wants you to come in four days a week (remote one day), so you are aware that remote work is at least possible. But you would like to come only two days a week for biweekly team meetings (remote three days).

From there, the next step is to tap into your agency, which is where your power lies in the negotiation. What is it about you that will make your manager amenable to your terms? That power could rest in your position, your performance, or a strong talent needed by the organization. Or it could just rest in your ability to craft a solution agreeable to both you and the powers that be. For example, Dr. Charis crafted a solution that would allow her in her role as a physician to also be able to take on speaking engagements, simply by not seeing patients on Fridays.

Returning to our remote work example, let's say your current employer allows you to work remotely two days a week. That alone, plus the fact that the company has chosen to hire you, is where your agency would lie in this scenario. When you focus on your agency, ask yourself what you can leverage and work from that foundation.

When you negotiate, understand that there are two primary ways of negotiating: distributive and integrative.[122] Integrative tactics aim to create value and find mutually beneficial solutions that satisfy the needs and interests of both parties. In short, the object is to create a win-win. Distributive tactics, however, focus on getting as much as possible at the expense of the other party, creating a competitive and adversarial atmosphere. Integrative negotiating is what I believe in and what I'm talking about here. It's healthier for all concerned and is the best bet to avoid an unpleasant standoff.

BUILDING RELATIONSHIPS

For integrative negotiating to work, the next step in the process (building relationships) is essential. Vipula Gandhi, a senior consultant and the highest-ranking female executive at Gallup, puts it this way: "Negotiation actually starts with listening and trying to get to a win-win. Listening is essential because everything about negotiation is understanding the other party. The person on the other side is also a human being, so ultimately, negotiation is about creating a connection and understanding their needs."

A negotiation is always a situation that rests on interdependence. You want to gain something you can't get by yourself, and someone else has to make it happen. Understanding that interdependence is powerful. You need them, and they need you to accomplish whatever needs to be completed. As I mentioned earlier, it's always important to tap into the other person's perspective. That's especially true with a negotiation.

If you can understand what the other person wants, you can negotiate in such a way that you find a way to meet both of your needs and hopefully work toward an amicable solution. When you're negotiating terms to start a new job, hopefully, your new employer will value whatever motivated them to hire you enough to try to meet your needs because the best negotiation leaves both parties feeling good. This isn't always possible, but it should always be the goal, even if it takes some creative problem-solving.

CREATING A CLEAR OUTCOME

This final step in the negotiation process, creating a clear outcome, is crucial. Your negotiations should have a defined endpoint so that tensions don't linger and your issues are resolved.

You can expect your outcome to be one of three potential endpoints. The optimum is, of course, your dream outcome, your aspiration point, where you get everything you want, or at the very least, more than what you consider your bottom line. Like most dreams, this often doesn't come true, but you should enter any negotiation with your dream outcome and your bottom limit, also called your reservation point, clearly defined in your mind. In our hypothetical example, imagine your current employer allows you to work remotely two days a week. This would be your reservation point because you are unwilling to accept fewer remote days than you currently have. However, you also have a fully remote job offer on the table. This is what's called your BATNA.

BATNA stands for your Best Alternative to a Negotiated Agreement. It's what you will do if you don't get what you want. Do you want to try to line up another opportunity somewhere else?

Are you willing to live without working remotely? Is there another path within the organization to get what you want? Whatever your situation is, you want to craft your BATNA in advance and have it in mind when you negotiate so that you don't get too rattled if you're shut down. Instead, you will already have a plan B in place. The stronger your BATNA, the stronger your negotiation position. This is a great cheat code because when you're prepared for any outcome, that keeps you strong.

🔒 **UNSPOKEN RULE:**

The stronger your plan B, the stronger your negotiating power.

The next type of outcome is more complex because it falls into what's called the Zone of Possible Agreement or ZOPA. ZOPA is the area where the negotiating parties' desires and limits intersect. For you, it will lie between your aspiration point (three days remote) and your reservation point (two days remote), where your bottom limit is. The area between those two points is where negotiating can happen. Through the initial back-and-forth of negotiating, you will hopefully be able to discern where the ZOPA is for each of you and start narrowing down the differences. Maybe you can work remotely two days a week but come in an extra day to meet with your supervisors twice a month. When you know what's possible and what's not, you can further focus your efforts on offering productive proposals that won't be dismissed.

But what if the manager is unwilling to budge on one day a week (reservation point) and your reservation point is still the two days a week you have in your current job? When that happens, there is no ZOPA, so you would likely be unable to find a mutually agreeable solution.

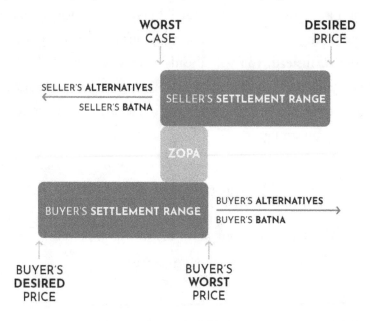

The Zone of Possible Agreement (BATNA: Best Alternative to a Negotiated Agreement)

That leads us to the last type of outcome when you or the other party walk away because reconciliation doesn't seem possible, and you've exhausted every option. This is where your BATNA comes in handy because this is when it's time to pursue your best alternative to getting the negotiated agreement.

Sometimes the best way to negotiate is to simply walk out of the room. Have you ever tried to unsubscribe from a magazine or disconnect your cable? Many times, they'll come back at you with a lower price, and you have to wonder why they never offered that deal before. It's because they didn't have to. People will withhold, because they're afraid they'll give away the store and give you too much power. Your job is to get what's reasonable and right for you.

You, of course, want to avoid having negotiations completely break down because nobody gets what they want. Sometimes, this can be avoided if you will, again, put yourself in the shoes of your manager or whoever you're negotiating with. At other times, you must craft a long-term strategy to get what you want rather than putting all your chips in one negotiation.

In my talk with Benjamin Collier II, he shared his view that negotiations should always be on your mind, not just when you're actively trying to get something:

I'm always negotiating. At my company we do midyear and end-of-the-year reviews. At the end of the year I spend a full day planning the next year; writing down personal, family goals, and career goals. From a career standpoint, I'm making time with my leader to walk them through my goals in detail, telling them what I'm going to achieve next year. I make sure those goals are big, they're hard, they're meaningful, and they add value to the organization. That way my leader knows that I'm bringing worth every single day during the first quarter of next year. Every month, I'm reemphasizing to my leader what I'm doing to achieve these goals, and I keep a detailed write-up of all the things that I have accomplished; therefore at the end of the year, I don't have to jog my memory.

Benjamin creates the conditions for a successful negotiation during his performance review. He's laying the groundwork all year, showing his manager that he's above average. That's a very effective way to negotiate without even negotiating. Because, in a sense, you are negotiating every day on the job simply by demonstrating your value through your performance. Many people don't see this aspect of negotiation, which can be dangerous. As Chris Voss, a high-profile hostage negotiator, says, "The most dangerous negotiation is the one you don't know you're in." That's why awareness is such an important component of negotiating.

Coping with Conflict

Of course, our psychological chemistry plays a huge part in whether we can negotiate successfully or not. Next is an illustration that demonstrates everything that's in play in our minds when we attempt to negotiate a win. Negotiating taps into your attitudes and personal experiences, how you feel about authority, and whether you feel you deserve good things. I'm not saying you must go into therapy just to become a better negotiator, but you should be aware of the factors that might be holding you back and try to get past them if you can. Try to be objective about the process and not take things personally. Negotiating is a skill like any other, and you can develop that skill.

Psychological Foundation of Negotiation

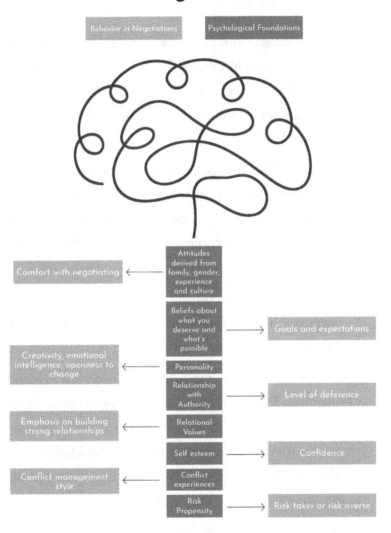

Naturally, all of these factors have the potential to clash when two parties attempt to negotiate. Your goals and expectations may be in direct opposition to the other party's interests. Your conflict style may be completely different from theirs, and communication may not be as effective as it could be. I'm sure you can see other ways conflict might be inevitable—the question is how do you manage that conflict? There are actually five different ways, according to Dr. Ralph H. Kilmann.[123]

- *Accommodation:* This is when you put the concerns of others before your own, like when you give up or give in to the other party. When dealing with an individual issue that you don't much care about, this is a good tactic to use in order to buy some goodwill.

- *Avoidance:* This one is pretty self-explanatory—either you or the other party is simply ducking the negotiation. This is a good tactic when you need more time to think, feel like you've been put in a corner, or you (or the other party) need a cooldown period.

- *Compromise:* This tactic will happen in a ZOPA situation where you need to find a middle ground, and both parties emerge feeling somewhat dissatisfied.

- *Collaboration:* This is the aim of an integrative negotiation, where you find a solution that meets the needs of all parties and ends up being a win-win. (Pro tip: If you do use this tactic, after the negotiations, make sure you emphasize to the other person what they've gained so that they can feel they've won the day.)

- *Competition:* This is the hallmark of a distributive negotiation, a tactic that should only be used carefully and usually as a last resort.

Some or even all of these five modes of conflict resolution can be utilized during a long negotiation.

Identity and Negotiations

Considering the potential upsides of negotiations described in this chapter, you may wonder why anyone would hesitate to negotiate for themselves. The worst someone can say is no, right? Not quite. As always, it is essential to acknowledge that identity influences negotiations, especially when bias is at play.

Bias and cultural stereotypes have implications for expectations of people's behavior (e.g., women are expected to be helpful and kind,[124] while Asian people are submissive[125]). When individuals act counter to those behavioral expectations, they can experience social (e.g., decreased likability) and economic penalties (e.g., lower salary) in the workplace.[126] Decades of research have evidenced backlash effects for women[127] and minorities[128] who act counter-stereotypically. Although negotiation is one way to self-advocate, it may be inherently riskier for certain people.[129] Social and cultural expectations can drive negotiation behaviors via two significant pathways.

First, when nondominant groups defy expectations, they may achieve less beneficial negotiation outcomes. For example, one study exploring race in salary negotiations found Black job seekers were less expected to negotiate their salaries than their white counterparts and were penalized when they did so.[130] Because women are expected to be feminine, they can suffer backlash, such as not being hired, being overlooked for promotions, or being judged as unlikeable[131] when they negotiate. The complexities of backlash build when you consider intersectional identities.[132]

Black women are expected to be aggressive, thus they may not suffer the same agentic backlash as white women or Black men when negotiating.[133] Likewise, because people expect lesbian women to be masculine, studies find they are not penalized as heavily for negotiating as heterosexual women.[134]

The second way these expectations impact negotiations is how people of nondominant identity groups show up to negotiations. Based on previous personal experience and knowledge of the potential backlash for negotiating, they may censor themselves or decide not to negotiate at all.

Serafina Smith, a Black female director in higher education, shared her experience with this type of backlash:

A few years ago, I applied for an assistant dean position, and the offer made was lower than what I made at the time. That triggered me to begin negotiating with the hiring manager. After sharing my counteroffer with substantial supported evidence and understanding of the policies at the university, the hiring manager responded, "I'm sorry if this means we cannot work together at this time. Maybe we can work together when another opportunity becomes available in our department in the future." During the call, I could sense her apprehension and frustration because of my request and counteroffer. Despite the backlash, I continued advocating for myself. She hesitated and sounded frustrated, but she said she would ask, and eventually, the result worked in my favor. I knew that I had done my due diligence to ensure I fully understood my options and the internal policies to help mitigate backlash in the request and firmly make my requests and counteroffer. After hearing the initial response, another candidate could have easily been dissuaded from continuing to negotiate. This could have led them to accept a lower salary for fear of losing a dream job.

As Serafina shared, many people from nondominant identities may choose not to negotiate to avoid backlash or negotiate for less. A study of white and Asian negotiators found that white women, Asian men, and Asian women reported less confidence and more fear of potential backlash and thus proposed lower first offers than white men.[135]

So, what can we make of this? First, organizations should ensure they have equitable systems for evaluating pay, performance, and other aspects of work vulnerable to bias. Next, leaders must recalibrate expectations and normalize negotiation and other self-advocacy behaviors for all individuals. They should educate managers and decision-makers on how culturally prescriptive stereotypes increase the potential for bias and backlash in negotiations and normalize career-enhancing behaviors.

For individuals, be aware of potential negotiation backlash relative to the dominant group. Still, in my experience, skillful negotiations often benefit you more than not. Data suggests by not negotiating a starting salary, an individual could lose more than $500,000 by age sixty.[136] Yes, the cards are often stacked against people with nondominant identities. However, negotiation can provide opportunities to influence the outcomes.

Other Considerations

A few other points before we leave this subject. In negotiations, you should examine the communication. How is the other party reaching out to you? If you're going back and forth via emails or messaging, it can often take the emotion out of it and keep the temperature low. You'll also have what both parties say in writing, which can be crucial.

When everything is discussed in person or on the phone, you lose that edge—which is one reason why many people, especially salespeople, prefer to negotiate in person. You may want to keep contemporaneous notes of those conversations and send a quick summary of points in an email to make sure whoever you negotiate with is standing by their words.

Equally important, be aware that time can be used as a tactic. When someone tries to rush a negotiation, they may be trying to throw the fastball past you. In that case, do what you can to slow things down and prepare a good response. Even though we live in an age where everyone expects instant responses to whatever they're sending out, don't feel obligated to respond to every message immediately. I understand the impulse to do this. When I was younger, I would immediately respond to everything to prove I was on top of things. Over time, I learned that led me to make mistakes or not express myself clearly. Remember, if you're at all unsure, it's OK to ask for a minute to think something through.

Finally, never take an immediate "no" as a final answer. Try to find out the whys and the hows behind that "no" and what could change at least part of that negative reaction. Maybe the "no-sayer" can't see alternatives or understand how your proposal is possible. Ask to discuss and come prepared with options you can explore together.

Things to Remember

1. Don't be afraid to ask for what you want. All they can say is no. But prepare the way for that ask, and do what you can to prove you deserve it.

2. Understand the ABCs of negotiation—awareness and agency, building relationships, and creating clear outcomes. Try to be objective about the process and not make it personal.

3. People may make assumptions about you, but a skillful negotiator is best positioned for favorable outcomes.

CHAPTER EXERCISE: NEGOTIATING WITHOUT NUMBERS

As I said earlier, most people think of every negotiation as involving numbers—getting the best price on something or getting a salary increase. For this chapter's exercise, I'd like you to reflect on your experience with a real-world negotiation that did not involve numbers but instead involved advocating for behavioral or organizational change. You might consider times when someone else was trying to persuade you to change or you were trying to persuade someone else. In either case, consider the perceptions and significant insights you gained from this negotiation, and analyze what this says about your style of negotiating. Answer the following questions to further your insight:

1. What was your goal? What happened in the negotiation?

   _____

   _____

   _____

2. What were the critical factors (e.g., power dynamics, cultural differences, communication platform) that affected how the negotiation progressed and your outcomes?

   _____

   _____

   _____

3. Who controlled the negotiation, and how did they do it?

   _____

   _____

   _____

4. What did it teach you about bargaining and conflict?

   _____

   _____

   _____

5. What were you willing to negotiate, and what was "off the table"? What was your BATNA in this scenario?

   _____

   _____

   _____

6. How was the negotiation similar or different from other negotiations you have participated in? What was your reaction to the results?

   _____

   _____

   _____

7. What surprised you, and what needed to be adjusted?

   _____

   _____

   _____

8. What should the negotiators do differently in the future, if anything?

   _____

   _____

   _____

9. Knowing what you know now, how would you alter your own and the other party's strategies to reach a desirable outcome?

_____

_____

_____

In our next chapter, we'll examine the benefits hidden in uncomfortable situations and how to maximize them.

NOTES ON NEGOTIATION

What is your conflict management style?

_____

_____

_____

_____

How comfortable are you with negotiating?

_____

_____

_____

_____

Are you a risk taker or a risk averse?

_____

_____

_____

_____

CHAPTER EIGHT

Lean In to Grow

Change where you are, not who you are.

–CAROLINE WANGA, CEO,
ESSENCE VENTURES

Discomfort is an emotion we've all experienced. Somebody says or acts in such a way that strikes us as hurtful or disruptive, and we're left not quite knowing how to respond. It can feel like there's no playbook on exactly how one should handle these kinds of difficult situations. This chapter is here to help provide that playbook.

Believe it or not, uncomfortable situations can be a sort of cheat code for promoting positive growth. I don't often quote the Navy Seals, but one of their main mantras is "get comfortable being uncomfortable."[137] They believe that when individuals and teams push the boundaries of their comfort zone, the more that zone is expanded, and the more they learn to deal with unexpected and difficult scenarios. That's why I advocate leaning into uncomfortable situations and, by doing so, learning how to address and even benefit from them.

Let me share a personal story that demonstrates this. A few years ago, I was traveling (as I do frequently) and sitting in the Delta lounge at JFK Airport, waiting for my next flight. If you've ever been in one of these lounges, you know that everyone's just doing their own thing. They may be eating, having a cocktail, checking stuff on their phone, or doing whatever to pass the time. It's usually a relaxed atmosphere.

But this one time, I began to hear loud sobbing coming from somewhere in the lounge. I turned and saw a Black woman who was crying loudly and painfully, and it was immediately obvious that she had suffered some loss. Why else would she have this extreme reaction in a room full of strangers? No one would choose to do that unless something bad happened.

For about a minute, everyone stared at her as she shrieked, "Oh my God!" into her phone in an agitated and piercing tone. We all began looking at one another, thinking, *Is someone going to do something?* Me? I had just gotten some food and sat down to eat it. I hoped somebody would reach out to this woman, but nobody did. This was peak discomfort, and nobody knew what to do. So, I finally said to myself, *OK, I can't just let this woman be in pain by herself. This is a moment, and I have to do something.*

To get this woman, I got up and walked across the expanse of this enormous lounge, passing about thirty people who were still sitting there and not doing anything. I went up to her, and wanting to allow her privacy, I asked, "Is it OK if I give you a hug?" I hugged her, and she told me she had just found out her best friend had passed away. That broke the ice. Other people approached, offering to get her water or whatever she needed. I sat down with her, rubbed her back, and told her to breathe and try to relax. Finally, some Delta staff came over to try to help her.

Again, this woman was a complete stranger to everyone in the room, including me. I wouldn't say anybody was apathetic about what was happening. And I'm sure all of us were feeling the same thing—*Was it appropriate to intrude on someone else's personal pain?* It also didn't help that she was Black. There were only about three other Black people in the lounge at the time. However, it quickly became apparent she needed some emotional support, and it fell on me to offer that.

That moment always stays with me, because it was a moment when I realized I had a choice. I could lean into what was happening or disengage like the rest. I don't tell this story to condemn everyone or to boast about my compassion. I tell it because it was a moment that helped me grow and maybe helped a few other people who were there. When we engage instead of disengaging from discomfort, we often open new paths and better ways of approaching situations.

🔒 UNSPOKEN RULE:

Opportunities for growth often hide in uncomfortable moments.

We all experience these kinds of moments, at work and in our personal lives. Often, there is no right or wrong answer as to how to respond to them. But if you choose to allow yourself to feel uneasy and work through your emotions calmly and clearly, you can be like those Navy Seals and expand your comfort zone. Niya Baxter looks back at the early days of her career:

Looking back on my career, there were many times when I wish I had the confidence to do something. And I do much more now. If something is egregious, I'll just say it makes me uncomfortable in the moment. If something hits me a little wrong, but I'm not quite sure, I will give myself a day to sleep on it. And if it is still bothering me, I will say something. I have found that actually being direct with people and having an uncomfortable conversation can lead to progress in the relationship. I'll put thirty minutes on someone's calendar, and I encourage my team and the women that I mentor to do the same thing. Find the time and have a conversation. If you don't it's just going to keep happening over and over again.

Speaking up can make a big difference in your professional life or, in the case of Chief People Officer Brian Baker, someone else's.

I worked at this company, and there was this area where only the C-suite executives sit. It was an unspoken thing. One day I noticed a new employee who would sit in this area. I started to observe how people would treat her and look at her. They'd slow down as they walked by, like, what is she doing? Obviously she was on the other side of some of these unspoken rules and not in a positive way. I said to her, "Hey, I need to talk to you." And I pulled her into my office and asked, "Do you feel like people are looking at you strangely, when you sit over there?" She said, "Yeah, I do." I asked, "Has anyone told you that that's where the CEO and his direct reports sit when they're in town?" She said no. I said, "I just wanted to tell you that because I have seen and observed how people are looking at you, and I think that must feel uncomfortable." I just wanted to be honest. It takes a little bit of courage, but it's not really courage. It's actually knowing how to have an uncomfortable conversation with finesse. She showed deep gratitude for that conversation. The connectedness, the humanity of that moment of that really was special. When you see something, do something.

The Positives of Negatives

Allowing uncomfortable or conflict situations to fester in the workplace can have some problematic outcomes, which include decreased cohesiveness and productivity, employee turnover, divided teams with strained relationships, and unhealthy confrontations.[138] These huge negatives develop because of permitting tensions to rise and not resolving conflicts in a timely fashion. The only way to combat these kinds of negatives is to lean in and be positive and proactive about mitigating them.

For example, let's tackle the ultimate negative for anyone in a job—failure. When you're told you're not delivering what your position requires, it's easy to fall prey to depression, humiliation, and embarrassment. Many people early in their career find themselves put on what's called a performance improvement plan, or PIP, providing clear criteria for improvement. Some people see this sort of professional smackdown as a death sentence for their career, but it doesn't have to be. In fact, a PIP can be an opportunity to take stock of where you're falling short and follow what's almost a road map to help you turn things around. Kimberly Hogg Massey expressed this view of PIPs:

I personally think a performance improvement plan is the best thing that can happen to someone. I think it's a blessing. Because whether you feel it's justified or not, there's a little truth in everything. I've mentored several people put on a PIP, and I've even had to put people on them myself. I tell people—you need to go back to your boss within a day or two and show them what your plan is. It's easy to say, "This person just doesn't like me" or whatever, but most times PIPs are justified. And your perspective should be, "If I want to stay here, I need to put my best foot forward and show them that."

As Kimberly went on to tell me, there are only two ways out of a PIP. You either lean in or lean out, meaning you either embrace it or walk away, in which case you'll probably be asked to leave the organization. While every situation is different, walking away simply because of a PIP is probably the wrong choice. Even though being put on one can be incredibly uncomfortable, it can also be an amazing opportunity to understand precisely where and how you need to elevate yourself in your professional capacity.

That's not to say bias doesn't happen, especially if you have a nondominant identity. However, Kimberly also makes a good point that there's usually *something* to a PIP. For example, research confirms that when a Black person is late, it's viewed much differently than when a white person is late[139]—the white person gets a lot more slack in that situation. It's unfair, for sure. But maybe the answer is to make timeliness one of your core work values, so you take the issue off the table. That way you're not excusing the bias; you're rising above it.

🔒 UNSPOKEN RULE:

Negative feedback can be a blueprint for growth.

Viewing challenges and roadblocks in our professional lives as being a hard-and-fast negative is a limited perspective preventing you from growing. I learned early on that, even though you might be angry, moving forward proactively requires stepping outside that emotion and solving the problem rather than dwelling on it. For example, when I was a young intern, I thought my boss, a Black woman, was picking on me by giving me a bad performance evaluation. She felt I could be more engaged with the team socially. I felt like she didn't like me because I knew I was doing everything by the book.

But, as we discussed in the last chapter, most jobs involve going beyond the basics. I was not observing some unwritten rules. For example, I had a habit of leaving social events early because I did not view those events as part of my job, mainly because nobody told me they were part of my job! So, she chose to teach me the unspoken rules via negative broad feedback. That wasn't the most constructive way to deliver the message, yet, ultimately, she was trying to help me develop and teach me the rules of the corporate game. I got over myself and learned from it. As a result, she asked me to work for her in a full-time job after my internship was up.

Doing What You Don't Want to Do

We all face situations on the job where we're asked to do something we don't want to do. Your boss might give you a task that's not part of your job description, or you might be asked to attend a conference out of town when you have other plans back home. Maybe your work team sticks you with preparing a presentation you don't want to put together. These asks can make you feel uncomfortable. Should you complain? Try to get somebody else to do it? Outright refuse?

Again, just like with a PIP, it's easy to look at these situations negatively. And, yes, sometimes you must push back. But maybe stop and think before you do because if you view these kinds of requests as opportunities rather than unwanted obligations, you'll discover they can benefit you in the long run, just like a PIP can.

Omar Wilson, another professional who's made his mark in corporate America, told me about an instance where he absolutely did not want to assume a role he was asked to take on. He was over DEI in his day job and was also asked to lead the ERG. "I was asked to be the head of our diversity and inclusion council by the HR director. And I sat down and told them, 'I'm already doing this. I think you should allow someone else to step in this council role because this is the work that I already get paid to do.' I basically turned it down, because it did not align with the strategy of where I wanted to go next." That was understandable, and it did not hurt his career one bit. But later in the interview, he told me that the same ask would represent a good opportunity for someone newer to the organization to network.

That's why you should be thoughtful about your nos. For Omar, there was nothing to lose by saying no, but for another person who was newer to the company, there may have been something significant to gain. For his part, Omar created his own unique opportunity that fulfilled his ambitions at that stage of his career:

A personal goal of mine was to network with executive committee members. I wanted the CEO and CFO to know my name. But I also wanted to be at the table with them as a thought partner. So, I got approval to create a video podcast that interviews our senior leaders. When I started it, people had left the organization because they didn't feel connected to the company or know the senior leaders. I thought the video podcast would enable everyone to see our senior leaders in a light they would never otherwise experience. Employees could hear leadership's views on the organization, DEI, and what's important to them per-sonally and professionally. The podcast enabled me to meet with almost all of the executive committee. If I had asked my manager, "Hey, I'd love for you to connect me to the CEO," it never would have happened. My manager may not even feel comfortable reaching out to the CEO. Now I am in a situation where, if I want to, I can text our CEO, which is an opportunity that most people, including many managers, do not have.

Omar found a different way to contribute that also fulfilled his desire to connect with his company's cream of the crop. He let one opportunity go by but didn't stop with that "no." He instead made his own unique path to interacting with the C-suite, creating his own niche, as we explored in the previous chapter.

There was a time early in my career where I didn't say no, but I might as well have. I was asked to support the head of our division in rolling out a new go-to-market strategy. Since I was responsible for delivering a certain number of billable hours per year, I worried that taking on this extra work would get in the way of helping me achieve that benchmark. So, I only did what I needed to do.

What I missed about this opportunity was that I was working hand in hand with a very important person in the company. If I had the benefit of a little more experience, I would have seen this as an opening to really connect with him. But my attitude was wrong. I only saw the project as an extra burden and never considered how I could use this experience for my long-term benefit. As a result, I didn't grow in that opportunity planted right in front of me.

🔒 UNSPOKEN RULE:

A strategic no will make space for a meaningful yes.

Nobody likes more work added to their day. In my case, however, it could have opened up some doors for me if I had bothered to "work the room" as I should have. That's why I advise you to step back from your emotions and look at these requests as objectively as possible. Be thoughtful about your nos. Look for opportunities. If they aren't there for you, try to create one, as Omar did.

Just as you should objectively analyze an opportunity offered, you should also be open to change when it happens within your organization. Change frequently fails at a company because people don't understand the mindset and perspective of leadership. Instead, they tend to dwell on the negatives of what the change means for them. It feels like a disruption of their comfort zone, in which things are done a certain way, and everyone is used to those processes. They may not be against change in general, but they don't understand or are worried about the impact on them personally. Fear of the unknown is huge, and who knows what's around the corner after the change is implemented?

If change is coming and you feel threatened, take a step back and think honestly about what makes you most uncomfortable with the change. You might even find an opportunity to talk to someone senior who can explain the management perspective on the new parameters. Not only will you get some insight, but you'll also get some bonding time with that person.

Things to Remember

1. Discomfort, if handled correctly, can be a cheat code to positive growth. No true progress comes without some pain.

2. Sometimes an unwanted request can actually be transformed into a great opportunity. And sometimes, if it's unfair and forces you to do more work without much reward, it should be avoided.

3. Your nos and your yesses should be part of your strategic growth, so be thoughtful about both.

CHAPTER EXERCISE: HOW DO YOU HANDLE DISCOMFORT?

As this chapter states, leaning into uncomfortable moments is key to professional growth. With that in mind, I ask you to consider one way to push yourself out of your comfort zone professionally. Whether it's taking on a new project, learning from your failures and trying again, or identifying your fears, write down one way you step outside of your comfort zone in the next thirty days.

NOTES ON HANDLING DISCOMFORT

How can you push yourself out of your comfort zone?
_____
_____
_____

Potential new projects:
_____
_____
_____
_____

Failures to learn from:
_____
_____
_____
_____

Identify your fears:
_____
_____
_____
_____

CHAPTER NINE
Create Your Own Niche

When you're in your own lane, there's no traffic.

—AVA DUVERNAY

When you think about the most successful people in the arts, they all have a uniqueness that makes them stand out. And what makes them special can vary greatly. Back in the 1970s, comedian Steve Martin made his mark by being completely silly, while, at the same time, Richard Pryor triumphed by tapping into his own personal pain.

Today, Taylor Swift maps out her emotional journey through her music, while Beyoncé pushes artistic boundaries and delivers amazing and impactful performances. All four gifted performers found very different paths to reach their massive audiences, and all succeeded in their own way.

So, what does this have to do with you?

Believe it or not, my hope with this chapter is to inspire you to be like these superstars. Think about what you possess, either in your personality or in your abilities (and optimally both), that will help you deliver the most value to your organization and, in turn, be recognized and treated as a valuable asset.

It may seem a stretch to compare yourself to pop culture superstars and legendary artists. Still, if you examine your favorite ones closely, you'll notice that they bring something to the party no one else can. You also undoubtedly have something right now that's all yours or that you can acquire with a bit of directed effort, which can help you reach maybe not superstar-level success but a higher level of success and recognition within your field.

In the first third of this book, we talked about how to own your story and develop your strengths so that you can hit the workplace with a strong sense of self. In the second third, we discussed how to "read the room" in terms of being aware of power dynamics and personalities and how to deal with them. Now, in this final third, we're going to focus on your needs, what you want out of your career, and how to get it. That process begins with defining your niche and working it hard.

SECTION ONE

Developing your playbook starts with self awareness.

Look internally to understand who you are, both in the workplace and as a human being.

SECTION TWO

How are you showing up in the workplace right now?

Examine the ways you experience and navigate your current space with others.

SECTION THREE

Look forward by moving beyond what's right in front of you.

Develop your own playbook to build a career and a life that fits and nourishes the person you are.

Your Job Is More than the Job Description Says

For me, a big part of my niche has always been offering strategic help. The key word there is "strategic," as it doesn't do you much good to offer to do all the grunt work, unless it's an emergency. I look for opportunities that will put me in front of the right people, as I did when I approached Dr. Laura Morgan Roberts, who became an important mentor to me (a story in chapter 6).

That's one way I deliver value, a word that plays a key part when you create your own niche. When I spoke to Juliet Hall, she gave me her take on the importance of value: "If you want to be relevant, you have to be a person of value. In a corporation, you have to be willing to ask, 'What problem are we trying to solve here?' If you can solve some of those problems, you become a person of value which makes you relevant and necessary to the organization."

When you solve challenges within your company, it not only demonstrates your value to your manager and the organization, but it also allows you to swim in your own lane, if you will. When you identify and address a problem in a way that leans into your strength, you are seen in your best light. That means looking for opportunities to strut your stuff and jumping on them. For example, you may be awesome at messaging and marketing. If that's you and you hear the company is struggling with their social media content, that's a great opening for you to show your excellence.

Omar Wilson, whom I introduced you to in the previous chapter, agrees that creating your niche involves identifying the company's needs and using your unique strengths to help get them met:

The way that I've been able to find my niche in any organization is by understanding and identifying the different areas of need. Once I identify the areas of need, I find out, what the organization cares about. Then, I find out how to marry what they care about with my personal and professional goals and my unique skill set. For example, we recently acquired a company, and I recognized that the salespeople who are joining our organization didn't understand our methodology of selling. And so I inserted myself as someone who could bridge the gap for the new talent coming in. That helped me further to establish myself as a thought leader in sales strategies and also as someone who was able to integrate the processes of mergers and acquisitions. I think the biggest thing that someone, especially talent with nondominant identities, can do is pay attention to the needs of the organization and offer solutions based on your expertise. I look at my personal goals that align with the organization's goals, and then put my full effort into aligning my expertise with the organization's needs.

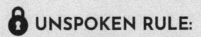

🔒 UNSPOKEN RULE:

Your job is always more than what it says in your job description.

One giant unspoken rule is that to excel at your job, you need to go beyond your job description and look for ways to improve the organization in a way that shows your value and creates a need for you personally. Show up as that person who can help in their own unique way and be useful to the advancement of the entire company. That's what elevates your career, not just meeting the minimum requirements of your position. "Just doing the job" may keep you in that position, but it probably won't take you much further than that. Anybody can do the basic job description. Not everyone can add strategic value.

Asking Questions

Juliet Hall also shared another powerful but simple cheat code that can help you create your niche. And that's asking strong questions. She says:

> *If you want to be relevant, master the skill of asking great questions early in your career. I have a coaching client who is struggling with his superior—and it's causing him to disengage. He's the smartest person in the room. Yet, he needs to find that pathway where he can manage his energy and his emotions and still engage. Part of my advice is to learn how to ask great questions. When you learn how to ask great questions is you give voice to whatever the topic is at the table. So that demonstrates engagement. People see that this person is paying attention. Secondly, when you ask great questions, you can shift the conversation and cause other people to reflect on the problem at hand.*

When you understand how to ask high-quality questions, it creates productive conversations and allows you to advocate from an informed place. The ability to ask the right questions that get to the heart of what's really going on without coming off as confrontational can help you unlock what's behind difficult situations and gain the keys to solving them. The key is understanding the difference between high-quality inquiries and low-quality ones. Categories of low-quality inquiries include the following:

- *Closed questions* that only leave the door open for a yes or no answer—meaning you've just given the other person the power to decide whether they are going to explain their answer or not. Closed questions are good for establishing basic facts but not much beyond that.

- *Leading questions* tend to present a viewpoint in the form of a question and can make the other person feel defensive. An example would be "You didn't see that stop sign, did you?" This indicates you already made up your mind about their actions. Leading questions tend to be based on an accusation or assumption rather than a genuine inquiry.

- *Forced choice questions* limit the response to predetermined options. "Is that a yes or no?" is perhaps the prime example of that. Survey questions, which also ask for a flat yes or no or may ask you to rate something on a numerical scale, are generally forced choice questions because there's no room for nuance.

High-quality inquiries, in contrast, tend to be open-ended and are aimed at achieving a deeper understanding of others' meanings and opinions. They encourage a challenge of your own views and are designed to expand rather than limit the range of responses. They encourage expressing diverse opinions, doubts, and concerns while simultaneously generating information for more informed choices and increased commitment. In the end, the right questions can lay the groundwork for insight and adoption of new perspectives.

The following are some examples of high- and low-quality inquiries.[140] You can see how the high-quality questions motivate more discussion and fewer brief and unenlightening answers.

Low Quality Inquiry	High Quality Inquiry
"Are you following what I'm saying?"	"What are your thoughts on the information I've provided?"
"Don't you think that's true?"	"From my standpoint, X seems to be the case. What's your take on this?"
"Did X or Y cause you to do that?"	"Can you walk me through your thought process behind that decision or action?"
"What's preventing you from doing X?"	"What resources or steps are necessary to accomplish X?"
"Why wasn't I made aware of this?"	"Can you help me understand the reasons behind your decision to not share this with me?"

McArthur, P. W. (2014). Advocacy and inquiry. In D. Coughlin & M. Brydon-Miller (Eds.), The Sage Encyclopedia of Action Research. Sage Press, 2014

Asking high-quality questions is especially important when looking for feedback from your manager or a client. If someone says you did a good job and stops with that statement, you should want to learn more. You want to ask, "What stood out to you and why?" or "What could I have done better?" to better understand what made you stand out and what didn't. The same goes if you're told you didn't do such a great job. While you may feel uncomfortable at the moment, asking the right questions about why you didn't measure up can be a massive opportunity for growth.

High-quality inquiries also help you better support your boss and your organization. As we discussed earlier in this chapter, the goal is for you to be able to identify needs and offer solutions whenever possible. Uncovering those needs and potential fixes requires thoughtful, open-ended questions that will elicit a deeper and more productive conversation and give you much more insight into the situation.

Leveraging Your Differences

The whole point of developing your niche is finding ways to stand out that tap into the individual strengths we discussed in chapter 2. That means not settling for just fitting in. If you just go along with the status quo, you don't distinguish yourself from anyone else. Many people in the workplace are too inclined to minimize their identities and their differences to fit in the culture (which is, more often than not, dominated by cisgender, white men). But it's more productive and impactful to leverage those differences rather than attempt to bury them.

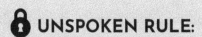

🔒 UNSPOKEN RULE:

The thing that makes you different could be your superpower.

For example, sometimes I find I'm the only woman on a team. If I dwell on that and continually tell myself that kind of situation is "not right," it will put me in a negative space. If I instead use that difference to uniquely position myself, then I can add value with the fresh perspective I can bring to the table and possibly open the door for more women to be in the room. When you come from a different background or have a different identity from the majority, you see the world differently. This difference can be your superpower.

You have your own vantage point to leverage and strategically use to help the team because you may spot a problem that others might not even know exists. For example, a marketing plan that aims to cater to women might need some important messaging or, worse, have the absolute wrong messaging. If I'm the only woman involved, I have the most authority to bring up the issue and offer alternatives. All people have blind spots. People from nondominant identities can help address those blind spots and add important viewpoints that contribute to success rather than detract from it.

That's why I advise you to operate from a place of confidence based on who you are rather than submit to who you think others want you to be. In chapter 3, I related the story of Marcus, who thought the best thing to do was perform as well as possible and never share anything personal with those around him. All that did was made him unknowable to the management, which subsequently passed him over for promotion multiple times. It was only when he decided to connect with people personally and share some of who he was that things changed for him.

Similarly, Donnie Bedney, a Black private equity executive who has excelled in the corporate space, shared with me that he found both freedom and success in embracing who he was:

Most people do not show up as their authentic self. I used to be that way. That changed when I got to spend four months in Nairobi, Kenya, serving as the chief operating officer for an HR technology start-up, and it was my first time living in a country where I was in the majority. Earlier in my career, I remember being warned about growing out my facial hair. My managing partner said, "They always say in business, you can never trust a man that you can't see his face." Well, in Kenya, I made a decision that I actually was just going to show up how I wanted to so I grew out my beard and hair. My experience living, working and doing business in Kenya allowed me to discover a side of myself where I could literally wake up and show up exactly how I wanted to. Now, I haven't worn a tie within a business setting for close to ten years.

When I came back to America, I had an interview with a large healthcare consultancy for a high-level role. I flew in for that interview, dressed as I normally would. No tie. My beard was long, and my hair was grown out. I ended up at dinner with four white gentlemen, which gave me an opportunity to discuss my experience and my qualifications. And the next morning, the guy offered me the role immediately, literally right in the interview.

Sometimes, even something personal that can be perceived as a weakness can be confronted head-on and turned into a positive. I spoke with Adam Rogers, a white executive who was diagnosed with attention deficit hyperactivity disorder (ADHD) later in life, to find out how he navigated being neurodivergent. He said:

I have struggled with ADHD in terms of when I should tell people about it and worried if they will understand. I've learned to be very open about it now, but I used to feel it was private. I had to have a growth moment to own it, embracing "This is just how my brain works." And if they want to know more, I can educate them.

I had to realize ADHD wasn't just a disability—there were some things about it that are very powerful. If I like something, I can focus on it. So, I tell people that I'm very good at learning about things but very bad at scheduling and showing up on time. I've had to do a lot of self-talk, framing it in my mind as something that doesn't need to hold me back as long as I put some checks on myself. It's not something to be negative about. It's just part of being me.

I advise people to learn as much about yourself as you can if you're neurodivergent and don't be afraid to advocate for yourself and to teach people. If you have an internal disability, it's hard for people to get it. But give them a chance and try—be open and comfortable with yourself. If you go, "Hey, I have ADHD, and this is how it affects me," I find they're happy to talk to you about it as long as you're direct and open to talking.

Adam's ADHD does bring him some challenges, but it also gives him a unique way of looking at things that turns his neurodivergence into a strength in his workplace. That strength is a true superpower because it's authentic. Some people build a niche that's artificial—

pretending to be something they're not. Sometimes you can get away with that for a while, but "fake it till you make it" doesn't really work unless you are able to reach that "make it" point, when you deliver the benefits you're promising. That's why you should always begin from a place of authenticity, taking your strengths and making them the basis for whatever you want your niche to be.

It's important to understand that nobody is indispensable. To illustrate that point, they used to say, stick your finger in a bucket of water, and then pull it out and see if it leaves a hole. The organization will always survive without you. But when you build a powerful and unique niche, you do create a specific role for yourself that no one else can fully fill. That makes you more valuable and raises your professional stock.

Go beyond the Moment

Finally, when you build your niche, permit yourself to think beyond where you're currently working and what job you're now doing. Be mindful of your personal goals, goals that may take you to another organization and even a different career path. In your head, you want to have a vision of the next stage of your professional development and lean into that vision.

That often requires separating your personal brand apart from the organization's. If you work for, say, Amazon, it's important not to identify too strongly with Amazon, at least not to the point where working for that company becomes more important than your development (or your sanity). When you work for a prestigious group or renowned brand, it's natural to feel proud, and you should. But that doesn't mean you can't work for a different organization, even a less prestigious brand, in the future. Who knows what you might accomplish there? Why put limits on yourself over a label? Juliet Hall put it well when I talked to her about this topic:

Don't make a company or even a title your identity. Throughout my journey, I began to develop a sense of pride in my position, and it got to a point where it was unhealthy. When you are at the executive level and you're making a lot of money, it does tend to elevate your sense of self and value. But when I give someone my business card, the value is not what comes after the comma. It's what comes before the comma—my name, that is to say, not my position. This was a hard lesson for me because the company that I worked for was a very admired brand, and I was almost hiding behind it.

You know you're in trouble if you place your value in your title, in the money that you make or the name of the company you work at. Just remember that the value is inside of you, the value that you offer to any organization. It comes through your strengths and your inherent God-given gifts. And it's really up to you to develop those—because your gifts will transfer to wherever you go because they're inside of you. Maximize every opportunity that you have at the corporation where you work, because they're gonna get everything out of you they can. So, you need to make sure you get everything out of it, to help grow your own human capital.

Along those same lines, remember that if you work for a big firm, they almost always offer many professional development resources that you can use to sharpen your skills, such as tuition reimbursement and certifications. I worked at one of these firms right out of grad school and have always regretted not taking advantage of those types of programs. You can also be thoughtful by joining employee networking groups and using opportunities to attend conferences where you can meet peers outside your organization. And then there are in-house lunches where guest experts offer insight into areas you may need to become more familiar with.

🔒 UNSPOKEN RULE:

Corporate resources are treasures—maximize them for your ascent.

Tapping into these kinds of resources is another powerful cheat code, especially if you plan on eventually going out on your own as an entrepreneur. When you do, you won't have those kinds of resources to draw upon, so why not take advantage of them now while you can? Maximize them to build not only your niche but also your career.

Where appropriate, also find ways to demonstrate your niche outside your current work environment. I just mentioned going to outside conferences when the opportunity is offered to you. Perhaps you can get involved with the organization behind these events or any trade association that represents your career ambitions. You can even create your own "mastermind group," which is when you regularly meet with a small collection of peers in different locations and different businesses, and you help one another with individual career issues and concerns.

Circling back to Juliet's story, I know how easy it is to develop tunnel vision where you are only focused on your immediate duties and whatever internal promotion you're working toward. But consider the value in devoting 10 percent of your workweek to external opportunities and networking. These activities aren't just about preparing for what might happen down the line; they will help you right now, in your current job, as you can tap into how other companies do what you do and, in the process, uncover new strategies that will help your team.

This makes you more important to your own organization. So don't think of looking outside your company door as being sneaky or disloyal. Leverage new contacts for your own betterment, of course, and also leverage them for the betterment of whatever organization you contribute to. If you happen to have a nondominant identity, external networking with those who share your identity will be of enormous value, because you will find out how others cope with how they are regarded in the workplace.

Things to Remember

1. To build your niche, think beyond your job requirements, and look for opportunities to fill other needs within the organization with your specialized skills and abilities.

2. Ask high-quality questions to uncover the truth about situations, and find common ground solutions, as well as position yourself as a positive presence in the company.

3. Don't hide your differences. Share and leverage them to create a unique role for yourself, and bolster your niche.

4. Think past your current role and organization, and build your niche externally so that you establish yourself outside your current company.

CHAPTER EXERCISE: DEFINING AND EXPRESSING YOUR NICHE

Jeff Bezos once said, "Your brand is what people say about you when you're not in the room." It's the same with your niche. Here are four steps you can take to both define and communicate your niche effectively in the professional world:

1. DEFINE YOUR NICHE AND PUT IT IN WRITING

What's your long-term vision and mission?

_____

_____

_____

What values do you want to embody?

_____

What motivates others to turn to you?

_____

How do you make a difference in your envirnoment?

_____

Create your own personal mission statement that answers these questions and defines your niche. For example, you might say, "My mission is to drive positive change in marketing through innovative and authentic campaigns, embodying values of creativity and collaboration. I aim to be the go-to person for impactful solutions, motivating others with my passion and dedication."

_____

_____

_____

2. AUDIT YOUR NICHE

Analyze where you are today with the niche you've defined in step 1. Do people really think of you in the way you want to be thought of?

_____

_____

Are you following through on delivering value?

_____

_____

_____

It's important to do some "market research" by asking some members of your key audiences (colleagues, bosses, teachers, family, friends, partners, etc.) whom you trust to be truth-tellers to give you objective feedback.

Who can you ask for objective feedback?

_____

_____

_____

3. EMBODY YOUR NICHE

Be aware of what impression you're giving others and what messages you're sending consciously and unconsciously. Align your communication with your niche in an authentic and positive way. Be wary of appearing too negative too often and instead signal positivity, productivity, and a desire to learn. Also, if you're heavily into social media, make sure what you're posting doesn't violate your niche.

Where or how can you effectively communicate with your niche in a positive way?

_____

_____

_____

4. CONTINUE TO REEVALUATE AND ADJUST YOUR NICHE

Your niche should always be regarded as a work in progress. With that in mind, regularly assess how your niche mission statement fits into your current professional position, and then tweak it accordingly. To accomplish this, you may want to repeat steps 1–4 on an annual basis.

In our final chapter, we'll look at how leaning into the conversations and situations you want to avoid can open doors to new opportunities.

NOTES ON YOUR NICHE

Who is one person in your current company or industry that has clearly defined their niche? How have they succcessfully done this? (If you are unsure, ask a peer or mentor)

_____

_____

_____

_____

_____

_____

_____

_____

_____

_____

_____

CONCLUSION

Write Your Own Playbook

Make your own kind of music.

—MAMA CASS

If there's one overriding theme to this book, it's this: You have the power to make the future what you want it to be. You can continue to learn, grow, and succeed throughout your professional life if you're willing to be thoughtful and strategic, work hard, and leverage your strengths in such a way that they continually raise your profile and deliver amazing results.

I am hopeful the preceding pages have revealed the unspoken rules and cheat codes that will help you in this effort. Throughout my academic and consulting careers, I've arrived at a place where I believe I'm uniquely qualified to speak to the structural barriers found in organizations and help people navigate them in a way that's authentic and self-empowering rather than limiting and self-defeating.

I've discovered over the years that my true passion is to empower people and help them present their best selves so that they are recognized and rewarded for who they are and what they do. I want everyone to understand they do have the ability to create careers that reflect their passion, as well as their truth and, at the same time, find ways to hold companies accountable for supporting the ambitions of those who are genuine in their spirit to boost not only their own agendas but also that of the organizations where they work.

To that end, when I began my nonprofit, the Ellavate Charity Foundation (ECF), I struggled to truly tap into what I care about. The problem is I care about too much. I care about mental health, I care about the unhoused, I care about DEI, and I care about creating progress in our society and in our business world. But I finally realized my unique skills were more aligned with empowering those who need a boost to succeed in the corporate space than anything else. So, I focused my efforts in that direction.

ECF's mission is to champion empowerment and equity for those who have been historically excluded in the workplace—through free webinars, community programs, and research initiatives. Our efforts support economic empowerment, professional development, and powerful networking for business professionals. We work to encourage good organizational practices by focusing on the impact of the corporate and business landscape on the experiences of historically marginalized identities.

I'm most interested in illuminating the unspoken rules and cheat codes of organizations for people who don't know them, because, as we've seen repeatedly throughout this book, mastering them can be the difference between making your mark and getting lost in the organizational shuffle. Make no mistake, these "hidden" guidelines aren't improvised on the spot. They are instead known to all of those who are a part of that culture. And they only work because people within these organizations have bought into them, whether they are right or wrong, fair, or unfair. On the one hand, I'm disheartened by that fact, because I really don't like a group mentality that dictates to those who aren't a part of the group. But in another way? I'm actually inspired, because there are ways to become privy to these secrets and put them to work as effectively as those who already know them. Perhaps even *more* effectively—as you can be more aware of them than people who are already a part of the established hierarchy and either only understand these unspoken rules on an unconscious level or take them for granted altogether.

In a corporate world ruled by IYKYK, you now have the knowledge. You know what these rules are and how they work. Your next step is to take them on in a way that's true to who you are while also serving your organization's need (or preparing to move to an organization where your own needs will be better served, if that's what the situation calls for).

When I reflect on my own professional journey, I realized how many unspoken rules I broke and, as a result, how many opportunities I missed. You may have felt the same way about your own career trajectory while reading this book. I advise you not to beat yourself up about those times when you "should have known" or "had no idea" (even though I admit that can be hard)—when you don't know, you can't do. Instead, learn from those moments, grow from them, and use them to inform your future journey.

Have a Major and a Minor

Many feel I've accomplished a lot in a short period of time. From my perspective, it could have happened a little sooner, if I had been more proactive in seeking out mentors, taking risks, and learning a lot of the cheat codes I've shared in this book. My career has been anything but typical, and honestly, that's what I love about it. I haven't followed a specific, carved-out path, and as a result, it's taken me places I wouldn't have gone otherwise. But most of it would never have happened if I let myself get too comfortable where I was. While I am passionate in my belief that work should be a comfortable *place to be*, I also believe it's important to challenge yourself on the regular and get out of your comfort zone whenever it makes sense.

I know it's not easy. When it came to starting ECF, I hesitated. I never sought out to be a business owner, let alone, also a founder of a nonprofit. But I saw it would take me where I wanted to go next and allow me to have the impact I desired. Never in a million years could I imagine half of the things I'm now doing, which is not only a little scary but also encouraging.

Which brings me to the title of this final chapter. Clearly, I have absolutely written my own playbook for my career. Currently, I'm a professor at a top business school, I run my own consulting business, and I am a thought leader in the DEI sector. If I had told people I would do all that when I was twenty, they would have looked at me like I wasn't thinking straight. I don't know that I would have believed all this could happen either. But now I am in my dream job (or jobs) as a result of following my own playbook. I can teach, coach, author books, do keynote speeches, and all the other things I'm passionate about. The power behind where I am today lies in that I'm not limited to only one of my many current professional roles. I wouldn't enjoy that. Instead, I'm able to balance my talents, expertise, and experience in such a way that it feeds all of my passions and professional goals in a way that I didn't even think possible until just a few years ago.

Perhaps the way to look at it is like this: Just as you had a major and a minor in college, you can also continue to have both in your career. Your major would represent your primary career push, such as your full-time job, while your minor could represent a different passion or interest. Using that template, it's easy to determine that my major is my faculty position, and my minor is consulting with organizations. One feeds into the other and makes me an overall stronger force.

You do have choices, but feel free to open yourself up to more than one. To me, that's a big part of writing your own playbook. The crazy thing is that many times, your minor will circle back to your major in some unpredictable way. Maybe you do stand-up comedy on the side. Perhaps you're asked to perform at the office Christmas party or some other special event. You would get to stand out in a completely different way and show a totally different side of yourself to the people in your organization.

In the future, someone might ask you to punch up a newsletter or help add some levity to a boring presentation. I've seen this kind of thing happen a lot, where an outside passion ends up benefiting someone's professional life, especially when they find a way to connect it to their position and their workplace. It only makes sense that when you tap into your superpowers, you can really make things happen.

The Personal and Professional

At this point in my career, I'm thinking about more personal matters—such as how I can make sure I'm taking care of my wellness and my family. Even someone who is as schedule challenged as me understands the concept of work-life balance. But I feel the more appropriate term is work-life integration, because the reality is we don't have one life that's professional and another separate one that's strictly personal. We only have one life to lead, and the personal and professional can't help but intersect. Do you not have friends at work? Do you not handle work on your off-hours? Obviously, the two must go hand in hand, and that should be taken into account when writing your own playbook.

Harold Kushner, rabbi and author of *When Bad Things Happen to Good People*, famously wrote, "Nobody on their deathbed has ever said 'I wish I had spent more time at the office.'" Perhaps that's true, but you don't also want to look back with regret at what you never allowed yourself to accomplish. The challenge is to manage your own mental and physical health along the way. For example, I once posted on LinkedIn a series of workplace "Burnout Awards" that people try to win that actually don't exist. They include the following:

- "Most Stressed"

- "Slept the Least"

- "Works While Sick"

- "First In and Last Out of the Office"

- "Works Every Weekend"

- "Never Takes Their Lunch Break"

- "Never Puts Their Well-Being First"

As I said, these awards aren't ever given out, except maybe as a joke at a corporate event. That's because the only "reward" you realize from "winning" them is burnout. So don't be fooled, because when you strive for these awards, you actually lose.

Here are the kinds of awards I strive for instead (and no, they don't exist either, but they should!):

- "Takes Breaks to Recharge"

- "Sets Healthy Boundaries"

- "Realistic Time Management"

- "Prioritizes Human Relationships"

- "Says No and Means It"

- "Actually Takes Vacations"

We are all a work in progress. Yes, productivity is important, but so is your well-being. One thing that has been especially helpful to me is doing a time audit study where you account for the percentage of time spent on things like work, family, self, and so on. When you see how you're actually spending your time versus what you value, you may be inspired to make some changes. I know I was! You can try it yourself at ellafwashington.com.

Looking Forward

Finally, I encourage everyone to embrace the future, not fear it. Workplaces are always evolving, and we have to evolve with them. This book has emphasized the need to deal with things as they are, not as we'd like them to be. When we fight change, we enlist in an unwinnable war, because change is inevitable.

Take technology. Right now, artificial intelligence (AI) breakthroughs have many of us concerned about our jobs and the possibility of serious societal disruption through misinformation and deepfake media. What often gets missed is the potential for AI to take a lot of meaningless and repetitive work off our hands and free up our time to focus on activities AI can't do—such as networking, creating positive professional relationships, and doing high-level conceptualizing and planning.

It will also mean incredible breakthroughs in all sorts of industries. One research study shows that 45 percent of total economic gains by 2030 will come from product enhancements, which will stimulate consumer demand. This is because AI will drive greater product variety, with increased personalization, attractiveness, and affordability over time. Expectations are for a $10.7 trillion uptick in global economic gains by 2030.[141] That points to more jobs, not fewer, being created by AI.

For those invested in DEI, the outlook currently is not as bright. Gains realized in 2020 after the murder of George Floyd have eroded somewhat after that initial flurry of corporate scrambling to boost nondominant identity representation in the halls of power, and the incident with Dr. Claudine Gay I wrote about earlier is a reminder of just how far we have to go. But that shouldn't put us back on our heels. We have made inroads, and we still need to continue to advocate for change. And you can still use effective strategies to navigate the corporate space while acknowledging structural barriers, create your own niche, and ultimately control your own destiny.

But let's end where we started in this book—with the idea that you must own your own story. That's where you should begin in terms of writing your own playbook. Aim for a real understanding of what you want out of your career, what personal strengths you can leverage, and how you can connect the dots of your education, experience, and achievements to reach your personal and professional goals. And, perhaps most importantly, try to clarify your overall mission and what you want to achieve.

Sometimes my students ask me what kind of jobs I think they should pursue. My reply is usually, "What are your long-term goals, and what roles will bring you closer to achieving them?" That match may not be 100 percent, but a certain job could give them the opportunity to build certain skills or exposure that could be important to their next role.

The point is understanding where you currently are, and how that fits into your bigger playbook is really important. You shouldn't just let your career happen. You should plan your path and travel fearlessly down it. What makes us different from previous generations is the fact that we have unprecedented access to an incredible amount of information. That gives us the power to be more intentional, simply because we can know so much more.

So, *be* intentional. *Be* strategic. *Be* in the next room before you get there. And even if you don't exactly know what your ultimate end goal is yet, you can know what kind of work you love to do, what kind of environment you want to do it in, and what type of impact you want to have. Only you can define what a well-lived life looks like for you because that definition is different for everyone.

Just know (as I'm sure you already do), there are always setbacks. There are always obstacles. Those are constants. But what's also a constant is who you are and what you can bring to the table. Juliet Hall, whom I've quoted elsewhere in this book, put it perfectly when she told me this: "A lesson for anyone is to remember the value you offer to any organization is inside of you. It comes through your strengths and your gifts. Your gifts will transfer to wherever you go because they're inside of you. No company can fire your gifts. Maximize every opportunity that you have where you work and develop your own human capital."

When you're writing your own playbook, it doesn't really matter what company you're at. It doesn't matter if you're not at a company and, instead, swimming in your own lane. Because your playbook isn't about *where* you are; it's about who *you* are. It's a living document that changes as you change.

What matters is being in alignment with your own self and your own superpowers and what you feel like you were put here on this planet to do. You won't acquire all that wisdom overnight. It will take some time to figure your goals out, and even then, some of them will continue to evolve. But if you're committed to this process and mastering the skills we discussed in this book, that commitment will bring you closer to getting what you want out of life. So, with that in mind, let's finish this journey, or at least this part of it, with one final exercise.

OWN YOUR STORY AND MAKE IT YOUR PLAYBOOK'S FOUNDATION

Use your history, as discussed in chapter 1, to look at situations where you've excelled in the past, both professionally and personally. Analyze what conditions allowed you to shine and which of your strengths were most important to your success at that moment. Also, note what was most satisfying about those positive outcomes and what aspects you might be able to replicate in the future. Conversely, also examine when you fell short for one reason or another. Try to be objective about the real reasons behind those disappointments. What was the cause of them? Was it a weakness on your part, the situation you found yourself in, or any other reason? In both cases, look for patterns that can help you identify ways to create more positive outcomes and minimize negative experiences. You want to tap into what works for you—and avoid what doesn't.

NOTES

Situations where you've excelled in the past:

_____

_____

What was most satisfying about those
outcomes?

_____

_____

Which of your strengths contributed to your
success?

_____

_____

Situations where you've fallen short:

_____

_____

What caused those disappointments (a
weakness, the situation, other reasons)?

_____

_____

_____

FINAL EXERCISE: LET'S CREATE YOUR PLAYBOOK

As I've said throughout these pages, it's important to develop your own professional playbook to meet your needs and find the best opportunities to showcase your superpowers. With that goal in mind, I ask you to take a comprehensive look at yourself and use the concepts from this book to go deep and develop your playbook for the future, keeping in mind where you've been, where you want to go, and how you can get there. Incorporate what we covered in the earlier chapters on the following pages:

NOTES

Past accomplishments: Where have you been?

_____

_____

_____

Where do you want to go?

_____

_____

_____

How can you get there?

_____

_____

_____

_____

ALIGN YOUR PLAYBOOK WITH YOUR STRENGTHS

Along those lines, as discussed in chapter 2, you want to ensure your playbook represents your strengths. Brainstorm ways to leverage your superpowers or aspects of yourself that attract people to your side to get what you want out of life. Also, find ways to compensate for or, when possible, avoid circumstances that shine a light on your weaknesses.

List your strenghts or superpowers:

_____

_____

_____

Identify your weaknesses or limitations:

_____

_____

_____

NOTES ON LEVERAGING STRENGTH

How can you leverage your strengths to succeed?

_____

_____

_____

_____

_____

_____

_____

How can you manage your weaknesses (so they don't hold you back from success)?

_____

_____

_____

_____

_____

MAKE SURE YOUR PLAYBOOK REFLECTS YOUR AUTHENTIC SELF

Chapter 3 talked about code-switching and looking for opportunities to click in the workplace without sacrificing the core of who you are. You don't want to arrive at a destination where you don't feel comfortable, so take a hard look to make sure what you want really represents who you are.

Identify situations where you frequently code-switch:

_____

_____

_____

How can you change those situations?

_____

_____

_____

NOTES ON AUTHENTIC SELF

What locations or situations make you feel most like your authentic self?

_____

_____

_____

_____

_____

What are some of your most valued core qualities or attributes?

_____

_____

_____

_____

_____

_____

PREPARE YOURSELF BY BEING READY, RIGHT, AND EXCELLENT

When you're aiming at your next professional advancement, your playbook should have a plan for how best to prepare yourself for that new and improved role. Are there other skills you need to acquire?

_____

_____

_____

Is there something else about yourself that could stand an upgrade, such as your professional appearance or approach?

_____

_____

_____

Create a realistic road map to make that self-improvement happen. As discussed in chapter 4, you always want to try to be ready, right, and excellent when an opportunity pops up.

NOTES ON CREATING A REALISTIC ROADMAP FOR IMPROVEMENT

What milestones or markers do you need to hit on your self-improvement roadmap?

READ THE ROOM IN ADVANCE

In chapter 5, we discussed the importance of understanding the people you need to work with and the environment you need to work in. When creating your playbook, you want to try to gain that type of understanding in terms of the future role you wish to inhabit.

What will you be expected to know?

_____

_____

_____

How will you be expected to present yourself?

_____

_____

_____

Do you see any conflicts in the answers to those questions?

_____

_____

_____

Now is the time to identify the gaps between where you are and where you're going and what you need to do to bridge them.

NOTES ON CREATING A READING THE ROOM IN ADVANCE

How will you bridge the gaps between where you are and where you're going?

_____

_____

_____

_____

_____

_____

_____

_____

_____

_____

_____

_____

_____

_____

BUILD OUT YOUR NETWORK

Whom should you connect with within your organization to help you advance?

_____

_____

_____

Who can be a mentor or advisor who might be valuable to your future goals?

_____

_____

_____

Which of your existing contacts can help you connect with those potential and valuable career guides?

_____

_____

_____

You will need support from others to get to where you want. Build that support early, using the cheat codes in chapter 6.

NOTES ON BUILDING YOUR NETWORK

Keep a list here of people you've reached out to and their responses:

_____

_____

_____

_____

_____

_____

_____

_____

_____

_____

_____

_____

_____

_____

_____

_____

_____

_____

DETERMINE WHAT YOU WANT TO NEGOTIATE FOR YOURSELF

Your playbook should contain what you want for yourself in a future role. Those desires may include a certain salary level and benefits, flexible hours, the ability to work remotely, or the ability to build your own business. Be prepared to negotiate for them using the tools discussed in chapter 7. Deciding what you want out of your work life, compromises you're willing to make, and lines you won't cross should be essential aspects of your playbook goals.

NOTES ON NEGOTIATING

What are your desires for your future role?

Which of those desires are non-negotiable?

LEAN IN AND LET GO

In chapter 8, we talked about discomfort and how it can throw you off your game. Think about the areas where you feel the most discomfort, and plan to challenge those feelings, even a little. Anticipate the kinds of pushback you might encounter as you lift yourself up and the difficult conversations you may need to have, and work on an approach to obstacles that empowers you.

NOTES ON LEANING IN

<u>What professional areas make you most uncomfortable?</u>

<u>How can you overcome that discomfort?</u>

<u>What obstacles do you think you may encounter as you grow?</u>

<u>How will you approach difficult conversations?</u>

CONTINUE TO DEVELOP AND REPRESENT YOUR NICHE

In the last chapter, you learned how to define and embody your niche in your professional life. Ensure your niche has a prominent spot in your playbook and is integral to your goals. Like your playbook, your niche may evolve over time and take you places you never expected to go, so be prepared to develop new aspects of your niche as you grow your career.

Finally, please remember that playbooks are meant to be guides to help you, not rules to live by. If you need to change course, either because of external circumstances beyond your control or because of an internal change of heart, don't be afraid to dig in and regroup. Your playbook only exists to help you find fulfillment in your life. And if it's dragging you down instead of lifting you up, it's time for a redo.

When I finished *The Necessary Journey*, I was hopeful we were on the path to a workplace utopiaTM where everyone can thrive, be themselves, and work together to improve. However the political pendulum might swing, I still feel confident we are on that path. I hope that the unspoken rules, corporate cheat codes, and tools I shared in this book have given you a sense of control over your own necessary journey, a greater sense of agency, and the confidence to advocate for yourself and the life and career you want. Because, like I said in the Introduction, our work does not have to break our souls. When you can thrive as your authentic self, doing work you love, it can fill your soul. That is my hope for you.

I wish you all the best of luck on your journey, and I also invite you to take advantage of the resources I can provide to help you on the way. Feel free to visit my website at www.ellafwashington.com for access to more exercises from this book, my blogs, and my contact information.

NEXT STEPS IN YOUR PLAYBOOK:

A. Identify 3 people you can share your playbook with for feedback (peers, mentors, Personal Board of Directors).

1.
2.
3.

B. Set one specific goal for yourself in the next three months. How will you achieve this goal?

C. Set a date to revisit your playbook and set an alarm on your phone or calendar as a reminder.

Date:

☐ Alarm set

ACKNOWLEDGMENTS

I thank God for giving me the vision and purpose to do this work of elevating humanity in the workplace.

Thank you to my family and friends for being the loudest cheerleaders in the room for me.

To team Ellavate, you are all the amazing force behind the scenes that make it all happen. Thank you for your dedication to our mission.

Thank you to my Georgetown colleagues and students for providing the space for many of the conversations that led to this book.

Thank you to each person who contributed to this book through your interviews, candid conversations, and courage to share your experiences with me.

To the Forbes team, thank you for believing in my vision and supporting me every step of the way to bring it to life.

Finally, I send love, light, and appreciation to everyone on the necessary journey for a more equitable and inclusive world. The journey is challenging, yet let us remain steadfast and undaunted by the fight.

ENDNOTES

1   "The State of the Global Workplace," Gallup, 2022, www.gallup.com/workplace/349484/state-of-the-global-workplace.aspx. Accessed July 21, 2023.

2   National Museum of African American History and Culture, "Social Identities and Systems of Oppression," Talking about Race, December 28, 2021, https://nmaahc.si.edu/learn/talking-about-race/topics/social-identities-and-systems-oppression.

3   In society, everyone is assigned multiple social identity groups. Within each category, there is a social status and hierarchy with dominant and nondominant identities. Historically, dominant cultural identities have had more influence and resources and granted privileges, while people from nondominant groups have had lesser resources and have often been systematically disadvantaged (racism, sexism, heterosexism, ableism, etc.).

4   Erin Freiburger, Mattea Sim, Amy G. Halberstadt, and Kurt Hugenberg, "A Race-Based Size Bias for Black Adolescent Boys: Size, Innocence, and Threat," *Personality and Social Psychology Bulletin* (2023). 01461672231167978.

5   Adia Harvey Wingfield, "The Modern Mammy and the Angry Black Man: African American Professionals' Experiences with Gendered Racism in the Workplace," *Race, Gender & Class* 14, no. 1/2 (2007): 196–212.

6   Daphna Motro, Jonathan B. Evans, Aleksander P. J. Ellis, and Lehman Benson III, "Race and Reactions to Women's Expressions of Anger at Work: Examining the Effects of the 'Angry Black Woman' Stereotype," *Journal of Applied Psychology* 107, no. 1 (2022): 142–152, http://dx.doi.org/10.1037/apl0000884.

7   J. Celeste Walley-Jean, "Debunking the Myth of the 'Angry Black Woman': An Exploration of Anger in Young African American Women," *Black Women, Gender + Families* 3, no. 2 (2009): 68–86, https://www.jstor.org/stable/10.5406/blacwomegendfami.3.2.0068.

8   Robert W. Livingston, Ashleigh Shelby Rosette, and Ella F. Washington, "Can an Agentic Black Woman Get Ahead? The Impact of Race and Interpersonal Dominance on Perceptions of Female Leaders," *Psychological Science* 23, no. 4 (2012): 354–358, https://doi.org/10.1177/0956797611428079.

9   Victoria L. Brescoll and Eric Luis Uhlmann, "Can an Angry Woman Get Ahead?: Status Conferral, Gender, and Expression of Emotion in the Workplace," *Psychological Science* 19, no. 3 (2008): 268–275, https://doi.org/10.1111/j.1467-9280.2008.02079.x.

10   Erika V. Hall, Adam D. Galinsky, and Katherine W. Phillips, "Gender Profiling: A Gendered Race Perspective on Person–Position Fit," *Personality and Social Psychology Bulletin* 41 (2015): 853–868. doi: 10.1177/0146167215580577.

11   Sandy Wayne, Jiaqing Sun, Donald H. Kluemper, Gordon W. Cheung, and Adaora Ubaka, "The Cost of Managing Impressions for Black Employees: An Expectancy Violation Theory Perspective," *Journal of Applied Psychology* 108, no. 2 (2023): 208–224, https://doi.org/10.1037/apl0001030.

12   Jennifer A. Richeson and Nalini Ambady, "Effects of Situational Power on Automatic Racial Prejudice," *Journal of Experimental Social Psychology* 39, no. 2 (2003): 177–183, https://doi.org/10.1016/S0022-1031(02)00521-8.

13 Audrey J. Murrell and Gloria O. Onosu, "Mentoring Diverse Leaders: The Necessity of Identity Work," in *HRD Perspectives on Developmental Relationships: Connecting and Relating at Work*, ed. Rajashi Ghosh and Holly M. Hutchins (Springer Nature Switzerland AG, 2022), 175–195, https://doi.org/10.1007/978-3-030-85033-3_8.

14 Graham Staines, Carol Tavris, and Toby E. Jayaratne, "The Queen Bee Syndrome," PsycEXTRA Dataset, 1974, https://doi.org/10.1037/e400562009-003.

15 Klea Faniko, Naomi Ellemers, and Belle Derks, "The Queen Bee Phenomenon in Academia 15 Years After: Does It Still Exist, and If So, Why?" *British Journal of Social Psychology* 60 (2021): 383–399.

16 Rebeca da Rocha Grangeiro, Manoel Bastos Gomes Neto, Lucas Emanuel Nascimento Silva, and Catherine Esnard, "The Triggers and Consequences of the Queen Bee Phenomenon: A Systematic Literature Review and Integrative Framework," *Scandinavian Journal of Psychology* 65, no. 1 (2023): 86–97.

17 Mary B. Mawritz, Johnna Capitano, Rebecca L. Greenbaum, Julena M. Bonner, and Joongseo Kim, "Development and Validation of the Workplace Hazing Scale," *Human Relations* 75, no. 1 (2022): 139–176.

18 Teresa Hopeke, "White Men Are Feeling Left Out of Diversity, Equity, & Inclusion. Why Should We Care and What Should We Do?" *Forbes*, March 30, 2022, https://www.forbes.com/sites/teresahopke/2022/03/30/white-men-are-feeling-left-out-of-dei-diversity-equity--inclusion-why-should-we-care-and-what-should-we-do.

19 McKinsey & Company, "It's a start: Fortune 1000 companies commit $66 billion to racial-equity initiatives," McKinsey & Company, December 4, 2020, https://www.mckinsey.com/featured-insights/sustainable-inclusive-growth/chart-of-the-day/its-a-start-fortune-1000-companies-commit-66-billion-to-racial-equity-initiatives.

20   Reyhan Ayas, Paulina Tilly, and Devan Rawlings, "Cutting costs at the expense of diversity," Revelio Labs News, February 7, 2023, https://www.reveliolabs.com/news/social/cutting-costs-at-the-expense-of-diversity/.

21   Rachel Minkin, "Diversity, equity and inclusion in the workplace," Pew Research Center, May 17, 2023, https://www.pewresearch.org/social-trends/2023/05/17/diversity-equity-and-inclusion-in-the-workplace/.

22   Tawanda W. Johnson and Julie Davis, "APS and partners help members navigate anti-DEI legislation," APS News 32, no. 12, December 7, 2023, https://www.aps.org/publications/apsnews/202312/anti-dei.cfm.

23   Minkin, "Diversity, equity and inclusion in the workplace."

24   Mitra Toosi, "Projections of the labor force to 2050: a visual essay. Visual essay: longterm labor force," October 2012, https://www.bls.gov/opub/mlr/2012/10/art1full.pdf.

25   International Labour Organization. (2017, February 23). Demographic changes leading up to the 2030 (Regional Perspective). Future of Work - Major trends: Demographic changes leading up to the 2030 (regional perspective). https://www.ilo.org/global/topics/future-of-work/trends/WCMS_545623/lang--en/index.htm.

26   Jeffrey M. Jones, "U.S. LGBT identification steady at 7.2%," Gallup, June 5, 2023, https://news.gallup.com/poll/470708/lgbt-identification-steady.aspx.

27   McCluney, C. L., Durkee, M. I., Smith II, R. E., Robotham, K. J., & Lee, S. S. L. (2021). To be, or not to be… Black: The effects of racial codeswitching on perceived professionalism in the workplace. Journal of experimental social psychology, 97, 104199.

28 Tajfel, H., Turner, J. C., Austin, W. G., & Worchel, S. (1979). An integrative theory of intergroup conflict. Organizational identity: A reader, 56-65. New York: Oxford University Press.

29 Dan P. McAdams, and Kate C. McLean, "Narrative Identity," Current Directions in Psychological Science 22, no. 3 (2013): 233–238, https://doi.org/10.1177/0963721413475622.

30 Maya A. Yampolsky, Catherine E. Amiot, and Roxane de la Sablonnière, "Multicultural Identity Integration and Well-being: A Qualitative Exploration of Variations in Narrative Coherence and Multicultural Identification," Frontiers in Psychology 4 (2013): 126, https://www.frontiersin.org/articles/10.3389/fpsyg.2013.00126/full.

31 Lauren L. Mitchell, Jonathan M. Adler, Johanna Carlsson, Py Liv Eriksson, Moin Syed, "A Conceptual Review of Identity Integration Across Adulthood," Developmental Psychology 57, no. 11 (2021): 1981–1990. doi: 10.1037/dev0001246. PMID: 34914458.

32 Carl R. Rogers, Pscyhotherapy and Personality Change (Chicago: University of Chicago Press, 1954).

33 Laura Morgan Roberts, "Changing Faces: Professional Image Construction in Diverse Organizational Settings," Academy of Management Review 30, no. 4 (2005): 685–671.

34 Adapted from Ken Coleman, "How to create a winning personal brand," Ramsey Solutions, 2022, https://www.ramseysolutions.com/business/what-is-a-personal-brand.

35 Kim Scott, "Challenge directly and care personally. 302: How to challenge directly and care personally, with Kim Scott," March 28, 2021, https://coachingforleaders.com/podcast/302/.

36 Gray, A. (2019). The Bias of 'Professionalism' Standards. Stanford Social Innovation Review. https://doi.org/10.48558/TDWC-4756.

37   Jessica P. Cerdeña, Emmanuella N. Asabor, Sara Rendell, Tony Okolo, and Elle Lett. "Resculpting Professionalism for Equity and Account- ability," Annals of Family Medicine 20, no. 6 (2022): 573–577. doi: 10.1370/afm.2892. PMID: 36443090; PMCID: PMC9705046.

38   Leah Goodridge, "Professionalism as a racial construct," UCLA Law Review Discourse 69, (2021): 38.

39   Christopher D. DeSante, "Working Twice as Hard to Get Half as Far: Race, Work Ethic, and America's Deserving Poor," American Journal of Political Science 57, no. 2 (2013): 342–356, https://doi.org/10.1111/ ajps.12006.

40   Kenneth T. Wang, Marina S. Sheveleva, and Tatiana M. Permyakova, "Imposter Syndrome Among Russian Students: The Link between Perfectionism and Psychological Distress," Personality and Individual Differences 143 (2019): 1–6.

41   Caroline Castrillon, "Why imposter syndrome isn't all that bad," Forbes, June 28, 2022, https://www. forbes.com/sites/carolinecastrillon/2022/06/05/ why-imposter-syndrome-isnt-all-that-bad/?sh=4e7680002fa8.

42   Kevin L. Nadal, Rukiya King, D.R. Gina Sissoko, Nadia Floyd, and DeCarlos Hines, "The Legacies of Systemic and Internalized Oppres- sion: Experiences of Microaggressions, Imposter Phenomenon, and Stereotype Threat on Historically Marginalized Groups," New Ideas in Psychology 63, (2021): 100895.

43   Ruchika Tulshyan and Jodi-Ann Burey, "Stop telling women they have imposter syndrome," Harvard Business Review, 2021, https:// hbr.org/2021/02/stop-telling-women-they-have-imposter-syndrome.

44   Vinh Giang, "Where are you from?" Instagram, November 10, 2023, https://www.instagram.com/askvinh/reel/CzdmiQRve7A/.

45 Susan Sorenson, "How employees' strengths make your company stronger," Gallup.com, January 30, 2020, https://www.gallup.com/workplace/231605/employees-strengths-company-stronger.aspx.

46 Gallup, "Learn about the history of Cliftonstrengths," Gallup.com, December 1, 2023, https://www.gallup.com/cliftonstrengths/en/253754/history-cliftonstrengths.aspx.

47 Marcus Buckingham, Go Put Your Strengths to Work: 6 Powerful Steps to Achieve Outstanding Performance (New York: Free Press, 2007).

48 Brandon Rigoni and Jim Asplund, "Strengths-based employee development: the business results," Gallup.com, October 9, 2023, https://www.gallup.com/workplace/236297/strengths-based-employee-development-business-results.aspx.

49 Douglas A. Johnson, C. Merle Johnson, and Priyanka Dave, "Performance Feedback in Organizations: Understanding the Functions, Forms, and Important Features," Journal of Organizational Behavior Management 43, no. 1 (2023): 64–89.

50 Jackie Gnepp, Joshua Klayman, Ian O. Williamson, and Sema Barlas, "The Future of Feedback: Motivating Performance Improvement Through Future-Focused Feedback," PLoS One 15, no. 6 (2020): e0234444, https://doi.org/10.1371/journal.pone.0234444.

51 Steve McDonald, "What's in the "Old Boys" Network? Accessing Social Capital in Gendered and Racialized Networks," Social Networks 33, no. 4 (2011): 317–330, https://doi.org/10.1016/j.socnet.2011.10.002

52 LeanIn.Org and McKinsey & Company, "Women in the workplace 2023," October 2023, https://womenintheworkplace.com/.

53 Alistair Miller, "A Critique of Positive Psychology—or the "the New Science of Happiness," Journal of Philosophy of Education 42 no. 3-4 (2008): 591–608. doi:10.1111/j.14679752.2008.00646.x.

54 Nicholas Tapia-Fuselier and Lauren Irwin, "Strengths So White: Interrogating StrengthsQuest Education Through a Critical Whiteness Lens," Journal of Critical Scholarship on Higher Education and Student Affairs 5, no. 1(2019): 30–44.

55 Gallup. (2018, July 31). The business case for diversity, equity and inclusion: A perspective paper. Gallup.Com. https://www.gallup.com/workplace/242108/diversity-inclusion-perspective-paper.aspx

56 Tara Sophia Mohr, "Why women don't apply for jobs unless they're 100% qualified," Harvard Business Review, 2014: 2–5.

57 Aleksandra Luksyte, Eleanor Waite, Derek R. Avery, and Rumela Roy, "Held to a Different Standard: Racial Differences in the Impact of Lateness on Advancement Opportunity," Journal of Occupational and Organizational Psychology 86, no. 2 (2013): 142–165.

58 Anna Sutton, "Living the Good Life: A Meta-analysis of Authenticity, Well-being and Engagement," Personality and Individual Differences 153, (2020): 109645.

59 Deloitte. "Deloitte dei Institute launches uncovering culture research - press release. New Deloitte study reveals most US workers 'cover' their identities at work to their — and their employers'— Detriment," November 14, 2023, https://www2.deloitte.com/us/en/pages/about-deloitte/articles/press-releases/deloitte-deiinstitute-uncoveringculture.html.

60 Astrid I. Emmerich and Thomas Rigotti, "Reciprocal Relations between Work-related Authenticity and Intrinsic Motivation, Work Ability and Depressivity: A Two-wave Study," Frontiers in Psychology 8, (2017): 307, https://doi.org/10.3389/fpsyg.2017.00307.

61 Güler Boyraz, J. Brandon Waits, and Victoria A. Felix, "Authenticity, Life Satisfaction, and Distress: A Longitudinal Analysis," Journal of Counseling Psychology 61, no. 3 (2014): 498–505, https://doi.org/10.1037/cou0000031.

62 Ibid.

63 Katherine W. Phillips, Tracy L. Dumas, and Nancy P. Rothbard, "Why black employees hesitate to open up about themselves. Diversity and authenticity. Minorities hesitate to share information about themselves at work. That's a problem for everyone," August 27, 2021, https://hbr.org/2018/03/diversity-and-authenticity.

64 Ibid.

65 Amber Ruffin and Lacey Lamar, The World Record Book of Racist Stories (New York, NY: Grand Central Publishing, 2023).

66 Einar Haugen, The Norwegian Language in America; A Study in Bilingual Behavior. Vol. 2 (Philadelphia: University of Pennsylvania Press, 1953).

67 Courtney L. McCluney, Kathrina Robotham, Serenity Lee, Richard Smith, and Myles Durkee, "The costs of code-switching. The behavior is necessary for advancement—but it takes a great psychological toll," January 28, 2021, https://hbr.org/2019/11/the-costs-of-codeswitching.

68 "Labor force characteristics by race and ethnicity, 2022," BLS Reports: U.S. Bureau of Labor Statistics, (n.d.), https://www.bls.gov/opub/reports/race-and-ethnicity/2022/home.htm.

69 McCluney et al., "The costs of code-switching."

70 Amina Dunn, "Younger, college-educated Black Americans are most likely to feel need to 'code-switch,'" September 24, 2019, https://www.pewresearch.org/short-reads/2019/09/24/younger-college-educated-black-americans-are-most-likely-to-feel-need-to-code-switch/.

71 Jordan Reed, "Understanding racial microaggression and its effect on mental health," 2023, https://www.pfizer.com/news/articles/understanding_racial_microaggression_and_its_effect_on_mental_health.

72   Madeline Will, "Teachers of color get lower evaluation scores than their white peers, study finds," May 22, 2019, https://www.edweek.org/teaching-learning/teachers-of-color-get-lower-evaluation-scores-than-their-white-peers-study-finds/2019.

73   Eugene F. Stone-Romero, Dianna L. Stone, Mark Hartman, and Megumi Hosoda, "Stereotypes of ethnic groups in terms of attributes relevant to work organizations: An experimental study," in Diversity and inclusion in organizations, ed. Dianna L. Stone, James H. Dulebohn, and Kimberly M. Lukaszewski (Charlotte, NC: Information Age Publishing, Inc., 2020), 59–84.

74   Courtney L. McCluney, Myles I. Durkee, Richard E. Smith II, Kathrina J. Robotham, and Serenity Sai-L Lee, "To Be, or Not to Be… Black: The Effects of Racial Codeswitching on Perceived Professionalism in the Workplace," Journal of Experimental Social Psychology 97 (2021): 104199.

75   Costas Cavounidis and Kevin Lang, "Discrimination and worker evaluation," NBER Working Paper No. w21612, October 2015, https://ssrn.com/abstract=2669801.

76   Lee Edward Colston, "The problem with being 'twice as good,'" August 29, 2018, https://medium.com/@Mr.Write/the-problem-with-being-twice-as-good-1de095dcacee.

77   Cam Caldwell, Rolf D. Dixon, Larry A. Floyd, Joe Chaudoin, Jonathan Post, and Gaynor Cheokas, "Transformative Leadership: Achieving Unparalleled Excellence," Journal of Business Ethics 109, no, 2 (2012): 175–187, http://www.jstor.org/stable/23259309.

78   Scott Mendelson, "Black panther" broke more box office records as it topped "avengers," Forbes, March 26, 2018, https://www.forbes.com/sites/scottmendelson/2018/03/26/black-panther-more-box-office-milestones-as-soars-past-the-avengers/?sh=4f6f17f61d37.

79   Camille Lloyd, "One in four black workers report discrimination at work," Gallup.com, September 28, 2022, https://news.gallup.com/poll/328394/one-four-black-workers-report-discrimination-work.aspx.

80   Paige McGlauflin, "Number of black Fortune 500 CEOS reaches new record high," Fortune, June 26 2023, https://fortune.com/2023/06/26/black-fortune-500-ceos-record-high-dave-bozeman/.

81   Bailey Reiners, and Brennan Whitfield, "50 diversity in the workplace statistics to know," Built In, March 28, 2023, https://builtin.com/diversity-inclusion/diversity-in-the-workplace-statistics.

82   Ibid.

83   Rachel Gillett, "21 highly successful people who rebounded after getting fired," Business Insider, October 6, 2015, https://www.businessinsider.com/successful-people-who-were-fired-2015-10#julia-child-was-fired-from-her-advertising-job-for-gross-insubordination-9.

84   Valentina Sanchez, "Here is what makes workers the happiest at every age," CNBC, July 16, 2019, https://www.cnbc.com/2019/07/16/here-is-what-makes-workers-the-happiest-at-every-age.html.

85   Joe Andrews, "Working hard no longer enough to get a promotion. Here's how to stand out," CNBC, July 19, 2019, https://www.cnbc.com/2019/07/19/working-hard-is-not-enough-to-get-a-promotion-heres-how-to-stand-out.html.

86   Hans-Georg Wolff and Klaus Moser, "Effects of Networking on Career Success," Journal of Applied Psychology 94, no. 1 (2009): 196–206. doi: 10.1037/a0013350.

87   Victoria Brescoll and Corinne Moss-Racusin, "How to Walk the Tightrope of 'Nice and Able': Overcoming Workplace Challenges for Female Bosses," Psychology of Women Quarterly 31, no. 2 (2007): 217–218.

88 Robert L. Cross and Andrew Parker, The Hidden Power of Social Networks: Understanding How Work Really Gets Done in Organizations. Boston: Harvard Business School Press, 2004.

89 Nihar Chhaya, "How to figure out the power dynamics in a new job," Harvard Business Review, August 29, 2022, https://hbr.org/2022/08/how-to-figure-out-the-power-dynamics-in-a-new-job.

90 John R.P. French and Bertram H. Raven, "The Bases of Social Power," in Studies in Social Power, ed. Dorwin Cartwright (Ann Arbor, Institute for Social Research, 1959) ,150–167.

91 Bertram H. Raven, "The Bases of Power: Origins and Recent Developments," Journal of Social Issues 49, no. 4 (1993): 227–251.

92 Fred C. Lunenburg, "Performance Appraisal: Methods and Rating Errors," International Journal of Scholarly Academic Intellectual Diversity 14, no. 1 (2012): 1–9.

93 Mahmoud Javidmehr and Mehrdad Ebrahimpour, "Performance Appraisal Bias and Errors: The Influences and Consequences," International Journal of Organizational Leadership 4, (2015): 286–302, https://ssrn.com/abstract=3331818.

94 Jerald Greenberg, "Perception and Learning: Understanding and Adapting to the Work Environment," in Behavior in Organizations: Student Value Edition (Upper Saddle River: Prentice Hall, 2010).

95 Irwin Katz, "Gordon Allport's 'The Nature of Prejudice,'" Political Psychology 12, no. 1 (1991): 125–157, https://doi.org/10.2307/3791349.

96 Emilio J. Castilla, "Bringing Managers Back In: Managerial Influences on Workplace Inequality," American Sociological Review 76, no. 5 (2011): 667–694, http://www.jstor.org/stable/23019215.

97 Greenberg, "Perception and Learning: Understanding and Adapting to the Work Environment."

98   Chhaya, "How to figure out the power dynamics in a new job."

99   Ibid.

100 Lebene Soga, Yemisi Bolade-Ogunfodun, Nazrul Islam, and Joseph Amankwah-Amoah, "Relational power is the new currency of hybrid work," MIT Sloan Management Review, June 20, 2022, https://sloanreview.mit.edu/article/relational-power-is-the-new-currency-of-hybrid-work/.

101 Weldon Long, "Getting over your fear of cold calling customers," Harvard Business Review, February 8, 2019, https://hbr.org/2019/02/getting-over-your-fear-of-cold-calling-customers.

102 Tiziana Casciaro, Francesca Gino, and Maryam Kouchaki, "The Contaminating Effects of Building Instrumental Ties: How Networking Can Make Us Feel Dirty," Administrative Science Quarterly 59, no. 4 (2014): 705–735, https://doi.org/10.1177/0001839214554990.

103 Zameena Mejia, "How a cold call helped a young Steve Jobs score his first internship at Hewlett-Packard," CNBC, July 26, 2018, https://www.cnbc.com/2018/07/25/how-steve-jobs-cold-called-his-way-to-an-internship-at-hewlett-packard.html.

104 Katherine W. Phillips, "How Diversity Makes Us Smarter," Scientific American 311, no. 4 (2014): 43–47.

105 Miller McPherson, Lynn Smith-Lovin, and James M. Cook, "Birds of a Feather: Homophily in Social Networks," Annual Review of Sociology 27, (2001): 415–444.

106 Daniel Cox, Juhem Navarro-Rivera, and Robert P. Jones, "Race, religion, and political affiliation of Americans' core social networks," PRRI, March 8, 2016, https://www.prri.org/research/poll-race-religion-politics-americans-social-networks/.

107 Gov.UK, "Community life survey 2021/22: identity and social networks," May 3, 2023, https://www.gov.uk/gov-

ernment/statistics/community-life-survey-202122/
community-life-survey-202122-identity-and-social-networks.

108 Gil Troy, "Democratic debate: what Hillary Clinton can learn from Bill," Time, October 12, 2015, https://time.com/4069862/democratic-debate-what-hillary-clinton-bill/.

109 Deloitte. (2021, April 14). Deloitte remote controlled: Managing the 'anywhere workforce'. Deloitte United States. https://www.deloitte.com/global/en/about/press-room/deloitte-remote-controlled.html

110 Katherine Haan, "Remote work statistics and trends in 2024," Forbes Advisor, June 12, 2023, https://www.forbes.com/advisor/business/remote-work-statistics/.

111 Deloitte, "Deloitte remote controlled: Managing the 'anywhere workforce'."

112 Nicholas Bloom, James Liang, John Roberts, and Zhichun Jenny Ying, "Does Working from Home Work? Evidence from a Chinese Experiment," The Quarterly Journal of Economics 130, no. 1 (2015): 165–218, https://doi.org/10.1093/qje/qju032.

113 Future Forum, "Leveling the playing field in the hybrid workplace," January 2022, https://futureforum.com/wp-content/uploads/2022/01/Future-Forum-Pulse-Report-January-2022.pdf.

114 Ibid.

115 Michael DePrisco, "Council post: taking advantage of professional associations in every career stage," Forbes, January 25, 2023, https://www.forbes.com/sites/forbesbusinesscouncil/2023/01/23/taking-advantage-of-professional-associations-in-every-career-stage/.

116 The PhD Project, "Annual report," September 28, 2023, https://phd-project.org/about-us/annual-report/.

117 Kate Den Houter and Ellyn Maese, "Mentors and sponsors make the difference," Gallup.com, April 13, 2023, https://www.gallup.com/workplace/473999/mentors-sponsors-difference.aspx

118 Jan Torrisi-Mokwa, Building Career Equity: How Professionals and Their Firms Achieve Mutual and Meaningful Growth. Congruence Press, 2016.

119 Susan Stelter, "Want to advance in your career? build your own board of directors," Harvard Business Review, May 9, 2022, https://hbr.org/2022/05/want-to-advance-in-your-career-build-your-own-board-of-directors.

120 Massachusetts Institute of Technology Career Advising & Professional Development, "Three activities to start networking in a flash!," n.d., https://capd.mit.edu/resources/three-activities-to-start-networking-in-a-flash/.

121 Indeed Editorial Team, "18 non-salary negotiable items to consider for your new job," Indeed, March 10, 2023, https://www.indeed.com/career-advice/pay-salary/non-salary-negotiable-items.

122 Otomar J. Bartos, "Modeling Distributive and Integrative Negotiations," The Annals of the American Academy of Political and Social Science 542, (1995): 48–60, http://www.jstor.org/stable/1048208.

123 Ralph H. Kilmann, Creating a Quantum Organization: The Whys and Hows of Implementing Eight Tracks for Long-term Success (Newport Coast: Kilmann Diagnostics, 2021).

124 Amanda Koch, Susan D. D'Mello, and Paul Sackett, "A Meta-analysis of Gender Stereotypes and Bias in Experimental Simulations of Employment Decision Making," Journal of Applied Psychology 100, (2015): 128–161. doi: 10.1037/a0036734.

125 Wen Bu and Eugene Borgida, "A Four-dimensional Model of Asian American Stereotypes," Group Processes & Intergroup Relations 24, no. 8 (2021): 1262–1283, https://doi.org/10.1177/1368430220936360.

126 Laurie A. Rudman, "Self-promotion as a Risk Factor for Women: The Costs and Benefits of Counterstereotypical Impression Management," Journal of Personality and Social Psychology 74, no. 3, (1998): 629–645, https://doi.org/10.1037/0022-3514.74.3.629.

127 Laurie A. Rudman and Julie E. Phelan, "Backlash Effects for Disconfirming Gender Stereotypes in Organizations," Research in Organizational Behavior 28, (2008): 61–79.

128 Julie E. Phelan and Laurie A. Rudman, "Reactions to Ethnic Deviance: The Role of Backlash in Racial Stereotype Maintenance," Journal of Personality and Social Psychology 99, no. 2 (2010): 265–281. doi: 10.1037/a0018304. PMID: 20658843.

129 Sandy Wayne, Jiaqing Sun, Donald H. Kluemper, Gordon W. Cheung, and Adaora Ubaka, "The Cost of Managing Impressions for Black Employees: An Expectancy Violation Theory Perspective," Journal of Applied Psychology 108, no. 2 (2023): 208.

130 Morela Hernandez, Derek R. Avery, Sabrina D. Volpone, and Cheryl R. Kaiser, "Bargaining While Black: The Role of Race in Salary Negotiations," Journal of Applied Psychology 104, no. 4 (2019): 581–592.

131 Emily T. Amanatullah, Michael W. Morris, and Catherine H. Tinsley, "Punishing Female Negotiators for Asserting Too Much or Not Enough: Exploring Why Advocacy Moderates Backlash Against Assertive Female Negotiators," Organizational Behavior and Human Decision Processes 120, no. 1 (2013): 110–122.

132 INTERSECTING IDENTITIES. Intersecting identities is the concept that an individual's identity consists of multiple, intersecting factors, including but not limited to gender identity, gender expression, race, ethnicity, class (past and present), religious

beliefs, sexual identity and gender expression. https://www.psy-chologytoday.com/us/blog/understanding-the-erotic-code/201906/understanding-intersectional-identities

133 Angelica Leigh and Sreedhari D. Desai, "What's Race Got to Do with It? The Interactive Effect of Race and Gender on Negotiation Offers and Outcomes," Organization Science 34, no. 2 (2023): 935–958.

134 Sreedhari D. Desai and Brian C. Gunia, "The Interplay of Gender and Perceived Sexual Orientation at the Bargaining Table: A Social Dominance and Intersectionalist Perspective," Organizational Behavior and Human Decision Processes 179, (2023): 104279.

135 Negin R. Toosi, Shira Mor, Zhaleh Semnani-Azad, Katherine W. Phillips, and Emily T. Amanatullah, "Who Can Lean in? The Intersecting Role of Race and Gender in Negotiations," Psychology of Women Quarterly 43, no. 1 (2019): 7–21.

136 Leech Marie, "The million-dollar mistake: women fall short when negotiating salaries," Biz Women, July 28, 2022, https://www.bizjournals.com/bizwomen/news/profiles-strategies/2022/07/the-million-dollar-mistake-women-fall-short-on.html?page=all.

137 Eric Sof, "9 Navy SEAL quotes to improve your life," Spec Ops Magazine, January 12, 2021, https://special-ops.org/9-navy-seal-quotes-to-improve-your-life/.

138 Acruthers, HR Communication Handbook (Kwantlen Polytechnic University), https://kpu.pressbooks.pub/hrcommunication/chapter/managing-uncomfortable-situations/.

139 Aleksandra Luksyte, Eleanor Waite, Derek R. Avery, and Rumela Roy, "Held to a Different Standard: Racial Differences in the Impact of Lateness on Advancement Opportunity," Journal of Occupational and Organizational Psychology 86, no. 2 (2013): 142–165.

140 Philip W. McArthur, "Advocacy and Inquiry," in The Sage Encyclopedia of Action Research, ed. David Coughlin and Mary Brydon-Miller (London: Sage Press, 2014).

141 PricewaterhouseCoopers, "PWC's global artificial intelligence study: sizing the prize," PwC, https://www.pwc.com/gx/en/issues/data-and-analytics/publications/artificial-intelligence-study.html.

APPENDIX OF UNSPOKEN RULES

UNSPOKEN RULE

Who you are *outside of* work impacts who you are *inside of work.*

Areas where your story differs from most of your peers are opportunities to get comfortable sharing some of the things that make you you. In order to be able to do that, you have to own your story.
Chapter 1: Own Your Story

Owning who you are gives you confidence anywhere you show up.

Knowing your story and understanding your identities can give you some awareness of why your experience is different and help you feel affirmed.
Chapter 1: Own Your Story

UNSPOKEN RULE

Success comes from amplifying your strengths, not fixing your weaknesses.

Determine how best to use what you've got to get what you want. It's time to uncover your superpower. Chapter 2: *The Power of Your Strengths*

Seek opportunities to align your work with your strengths.

Emphasis on your strengths empowers you to search for situations where you can make your mark and demonstrate the superior performance that will make the higher-ups see you in a new and more favorable light. Chapter 2: *The Power of Your Strengths*

UNSPOKEN RULE

Own your flaws, and turn stumbling blocks into stepping stones for success.

Be aware of and manage your weaknesses so that they don't prevent you from succeeding.
Chapter 2: *The Power of Your Strengths*

Success is a team sport. Every star had a wingman or backstage hero who made the win possible.

The idea that people make it entirely on their own is a myth that robs many deserving people of their chance to take their strengths as far as they can go.
Chapter 2: *The Power of Your Strengths*

UNSPOKEN RULE

Everyone code-switches at work (to some degree).

Almost everyone struggles with authenticity in the workplace, not just people with nondominant identities. Chapter 3: *Authenticity and Code-Switching*

Code-switching can be a strategy.

Properly deployed, code-switching is a cheat code that empowers you to connect with different people in different ways. Chapter 3: *Authenticity and Code-Switching*

UNSPOKEN RULE

Strong workplace relationships pave the way to success.

Have an intention to build relationships on the job. You don't have to be best friends. You can still create a connection that will help you bridge your differences. Chapter 3: *Authenticity and Code-Switching*

Excellence does not mean perfection. It means doing your personal best.

Nobody can be perfect. Unfortunately, people sometimes confuse excellence with perfection, when it is more about doing the job as well as we can whenever we can. Chapter 4: *Be Ready, Be Right, Be Excellent*

UNSPOKEN RULE

Make sure you always have the receipts.

You must have your ducks in a row when you have a nondominant identity, and you should always have receipts.
Chapter 4: *Be Ready, Be Right, Be Excellent*

Delivering your best helps you navigate shifting expectations.

It can be difficult, but you can transcend a negative work experience if you don't give up on yourself. Instead, focus on creating your own opportunities for success in ways that suit your talents and temperament.
Chapter 4: *Be Ready, Be Right, Be Excellent*

UNSPOKEN RULE

Work in a way where you will get recognized for it.

No matter how hard you work, if you keep your head in the sand, corporate America may not notice. You don't have to do jumping jacks in the break room to get people's attention, but you don't want to be shy about taking credit for something you've accomplished. Chapter 4: Be Ready, Be Right, Be Excellent

What's not said is often more important than what is said.

Learning to read the room helps you be more prepared, less surprised, more action oriented, and less emotional. It allows you to make more informed decisions that reflect the reality of the situation. Chapter 5: Read the Room

UNSPOKEN RULE

"Doing your job" only gets you so far.

You also have to be strategic with your relationships. Otherwise, you will reach a point where your career may stall.
Chapter 5: *Read the Room*

Power in the workplace goes beyond titles; it's also about success, resources, and relationships that allow you to get things done.

Power is never evenly distributed, nor is it dependent on what's put on paper. Power is always relative, fluid, and changing.
Chapter 5: *Read the Room*

UNSPOKEN RULE

If you want something, you must ask for it, even if it's uncomfortable.

Instead of looking at potential rejection, focus on the positive possibilities, and it could be a game changer.
Chapter 6: *Expand Your Networks of Influence*

It's not *what* you know but *who* you know.

Being comfortable reaching out to new people is half the battle of expanding your network. Intentionally building relationships across differences can be a game changer in the workplace.
Chapter 6: *Expand Your Networks of Influence*

UNSPOKEN RULE

Embracing invitations to build connections can unlock opportunities.

Diversifying and expanding your professional network is a pivotal aspect of career growth, and a highly effective avenue to achieve this is by actively participating in a professional association or industry group.
Chapter 6: *Expand Your Networks of Influence*

Inside information is valuable information.

Keeping up with people who impress you can be a blessing. They can provide important inside information that helps you avoid difficult situations.
Chapter 6: *Expand Your Networks of Influence*

UNSPOKEN RULE

Everything is negotiable.

Most of us think of negotiating as always being about the numbers—salary amounts, prices, discounts, and so forth. But there's much more to it than that. *Chapter 7: Master the ABCs of Negotiation*

Negotiations can happen at any point in the employee life cycle, not just during hiring.

There are always moments in your career after the initial job offer where you can negotiate things like job assignments, performance reviews, service work, your job title, your reporting structure, your exit package, and more. *Chapter 7: Master the ABCs of Negotiation*

UNSPOKEN RULE

The stronger your plan B, the stronger your negotiating power.

Whatever your situation is, you want to craft your plan B in advance and have it in mind when you negotiate so that you don't get too rattled if you're shut down. This is a great cheat code because when you're prepared for any outcome, that keeps you strong.
Chapter 7: *Master the ABCs of Negotiation*

Opportunities for growth often hide in uncomfortable moments.

When we engage instead of disengaging from discomfort, we often open new paths and better ways of approaching situations.
Chapter 8: *Lean In to Grow*

UNSPOKEN RULE

Negative feedback can be a blueprint for growth.

Viewing challenges and roadblocks in our professional lives as being a hard-and-fast negative is a limited perspective preventing you from growing. Moving forward proactively requires stepping outside that emotion and solving the problem rather than dwelling on it.
Chapter 8: *Lean In to Grow*

A strategic no will make space for a meaningful yes.

Step back from your emotions and look at things as objectively as possible. Be thoughtful about your nos. Look for opportunities. If they aren't there for you, try to create one.
Chapter 8: *Lean In to Grow*

UNSPOKEN RULE

Your job is always more than what it says in your job description.

To excel at your job, you need to go beyond your job description and look for ways to improve the organization in a way that shows your value and creates a need for you personally. Show up as that person who can help in their own unique way and be useful to the advancement of the entire company. That's what elevates your career.
Chapter 9: Create Your Own Niche

The thing that makes you different could be your superpower.

Many people in the workplace are too inclined to minimize their identities and their differences to fit in the culture. But it's more productive and impactful to leverage those differences rather than attempt to bury them.
Chapter 9: Create Your Own Niche

UNSPOKEN RULE

Corporate resources are treasures— maximize them for your ascent.

Tapping into these kinds of resources is another powerful cheat code, especially if you plan on eventually going out on your own as an entrepreneur. When you do, you won't have those kinds of resources to draw upon, so why not take advantage of them now while you can? Maximize them to build not only your niche but also your career.

Chapter 9: Create Your Own Niche